Young Writers

First published in Great Britain in 2004 by:
Young Writers
Remus House
Coltsfoot Drive
Peterborough
PE2 9JX
Telephone: 01733 890066
Website: www.youngwriters.co.uk

All Rights Reserved

© Copyright Contributors 2004

SB ISBN 1 84460 469 1

Foreword

Young Writers was established in 1991 and has been passionately devoted to the promotion of reading and writing in children and young adults ever since. The quest continues today. Young Writers remains as committed to engendering the fostering of burgeoning poetic and literary talent as ever.

This year's Young Writers competition has proven as vibrant and dynamic as ever and we are delighted to present a showcase of the best poetry from across the UK. Each poem has been carefully selected from a wealth of *Once Upon A Rhyme* entries before ultimately being published in this, our twelfth primary school poetry series.

Once again, we have been supremely impressed by the overall high quality of the entries we have received. The imagination, energy and creativity which has gone into each young writer's entry made choosing the best poems a challenging and often difficult but ultimately hugely rewarding task - the general high standard of the work submitted amply vindicating this opportunity to bring their poetry to a larger appreciative audience.

We sincerely hope you are pleased with our final selection and that you will enjoy *Once Upon A Rhyme Gtr Manchester* for many years to come.

Contents

Alma Park Primary School
Susan Maria-Dawn Wood (9) — 1
Caseem Parveen (9) — 1
Sarah Coppersthwaite — 2
James Samuel Walker (8) — 2
Kyle Paul Seddon (8) — 3
Sayma Shaheen (9) — 3
C J Hammett (8) — 4
Kimberley France (9) — 4
Rebecca Wrench (8) — 4
Chelsea Rhiann Marley (9) — 5
Mohammed Abbas (9) — 5
Jake Paton (10) — 5
Tom Patrick Cragg Bishop (10) — 6
Laveeza Waseem (8) — 7
Asim Saeed (9) — 7
Harriet Jessica Mann (8) — 7
Jade Appleyard (10) — 8

Button Lane School
Daniel Watts (8) — 8
Mark Hudson (10) — 9
Steven Dodd (10) — 9
Soraya Chiheb (9) — 10
Leon Potter (10) — 10
Kelly West (11) — 11
Andrew Chappell (11) — 11
Aimee Price (9) — 12
Natalie Sheridan (11) — 12
Alex Herd (7) — 13
Ryan Gillman (7) — 13
Laura Jane Fielding (11) — 14
Nick Morrow (11) — 14
Sophie Anne Dalton (8) — 15
Jessica Yiu (11) — 15
Megan Barnes (9) — 16
Mohammad Jaberansari (11) — 16
Chloe Potter (10) — 17
Anthony Stone (11) — 17

Rebekah Layfield-Cole (10)   18
Andrew Stewart (9)   18
Bethany Miller (8)   19
Ellé Bates (7)   19
Amy Smith (10)   20
Jessica Lee (9)   20

Chorlton CE Primary School
James Fisher (8)   21
Karla Murphy (10)   21
Rebecca Barber (10)   22
Nathan Dalby (11)   22
Lauren Newbery (10)   23
Bethan Ward (8)   23
Tom Byrne (10)   24
Connor Turner (9)   24
Kenneth Chung (9)   25
Hannah Miller (10)   25
Louisa Cole (11)   26
Saqib Ashraf (9)   26
Chelise-Ray Davies (10)   27
Emma Clare (8)   27
Callum Bird (11)   27
Amy Heathcote (10)   28
Matthew Charles Edwards (8)   28
Danny Vose (10)   28
Rory Jack McGagh (10)   29
Laurie Emma Micallef (10)   29
Oskar Sutton (9)   29
Adil Danyal Anwar (9)   30
Isabella Rees (8)   30
Dilan Mohiedin (9)   30
Florence Millar (9)   31
Stavros Sapountzis (10)   31
Talia Ogunyemi (10)   32

Church of England School of The Resurrection
Demi-Lea Fraine (10)   33
Abbie Sherwin (9)   33
Tasha Dodd (9)   34
Hanna Delaney (9)   34

Ashley Mottram (10) — 35
Kemi Awodiji (10) — 35
Lauren Nagle-Moth (10) — 36
Phillip Joseph Chatburn (!0) — 36
Patrick Souter (10) — 37
Darion Blackett (9) — 37
Danielle Purcell (8) — 37
Robyn Cannon (7) — 38
Jacquelinejade Mason (9) — 38
Naomi Yong (9) — 38
Charlotte Palmer (8) — 39
Kane Gardner (8) — 39
Rebecca Isherwood (7) — 39
Abbie Taylor (9) — 40
Chelsea Dunn Winder (8) — 40
Katy Chatburn (8) — 40
Edwin Nurse (9) — 41
Chloé Hoskison-Elliott (8) — 41
Kane O'Connor (9) — 41
Miqat Chowdhury (8) — 42

Crowcroft Park Primary School
Ruqayya Ashraf (9) — 42
Tristan Schofield (10) — 42
Georgina Grimshaw (9) — 43
Samra Tabasum (10) — 43
Fanika Saeeda (10) — 44
Danielle Anderson (10) — 44
Sinnika Bernard (10) — 45
Sana Rathore (10) — 45
Ikra Ahmed (10) — 46
Anahita Karimi (9) — 46

Denton West End Primary School
Ciaran Ryan (10) — 47
Amy Potts (10) — 47
Cu-Yeon Lee (9) — 48
Benjamin Lowndes (11) — 48
Phillip Jackson (10) — 49
Kirsty Smith (9) — 49
Eleanor Jones (10) — 50

Natasha Oliver (10)	50
Grace Alicia Higginbottom (9)	51
Joseph Carroll (9)	51
Christopher Hulme (9)	52
Dominic Pimlott (11)	52
Natalie Lovatt & Danielle Richardson (8)	53
Daniel Higham (11)	53
Luke Cooper & Patrick Lyons (8)	54
Melissa Wilson (8)	54
Rebecca Taylor (8)	54
Laura Jones (10) & Rachel Jones (8)	55
Sophie Rowen (8)	55
Megan Dowse (10)	56
Alisha Street (11)	57
Samantha Havern (10)	58
Thomas Barr (10)	58
Charlotte Dearden (11)	59
Thomas Ellor (11)	60
David Webb (10)	61
Rachael Postill (10)	62
Emma Raisbeck (9)	62
Isabel O'Brien & Katie Savage (8)	63
Rachel Nield (10)	63
Emily Haughton (9)	63
Philip Kinder (10)	64
Joseph Jones (9)	64
Daniel O'Connell (10)	65
Emily Boggia (9)	66
Callum Dickson (8)	66
Matthew Smith (8)	66
Kay Murfett (10)	67
James Scanlan (8)	67
Jennifer Cowell (11)	68
Sean Talbot (10)	68
Samantha Mitchell (10)	69
Amy Pratt (10)	69
Karl Fairhurst (11)	70
Louis Ferguson (10)	71
Faye McInnes (11)	72
Emma Schofield (11)	72
Victoria Hooton (10)	73
Katie Anne Lewis (11)	74

Charlotte Wilkins (10)	75
Samuel Layne (11)	76
Christopher McAllister (11)	77
Sam Burrows (10)	78
Erin Dickson (11)	79
Bethany Mullarkey (10)	80
Thomas Thorpe (11)	80
Charlotte Williams (10)	81
Rebecca Oliver (7)	82

Haveley Hey Primary School

Daryll Alladice (9)	82
Nathan Frazer & Steven Hayhurst	83
Chloe Pritchard (8)	83
Harlie Burgess (10)	84
Patience Owens (9)	84
Paige Dyson (9)	85
Jake Grady (11)	85
Adam Locklin (9)	86
Adam Mayes (10)	86
Lisa Bond (10)	86
Chloe Smith (10)	87
Ainsley Gittings (10)	87

Manchester Road Primary School

Joshua Butterworth (9)	87
Sophie Stockton (9)	88
Mully Kempson (8)	88
Jay Ogden (8)	89
Ryan Watson (9)	89
Danielle Scott (8)	90
Charlotte Murray (8)	90
Connie Blakey (8)	91
Callum McCartney (8)	91
Laurence Giles (8)	92
Christopher Walker (9)	92
Callum Olliver (8)	93
Alix Allbrighton (8)	93
Jack Barnes (9)	94
Lloyd Simpson (10)	94
Courtney Clarke (8)	95

David Broome (10)	95
Victoria Haining (8)	96
Amy Crowley (10)	96
Francesca Hodson-Ridgway (9)	97
Bethan Redman (10)	97
Kyle Howles (10)	98
Joe Blakey (11)	98
Jordan Thompson (9)	99
Elizabeth Fenwick (10)	100
Thomas Lawlor (10)	100
Rachel Hammersley (8)	101
Ashleigh Duty (9)	101
Ashlie Ball (10)	102
Christie Marsh (9)	102
Jodie Wilson (10)	103
Amy Schofield (9)	103
Rachel Gill (9)	103
Lauren Scott (10)	104
Danielle Kenny (9)	105
Dane Oliver (9)	106
Sarah Newsham (11)	106
Andrei Howles (9)	107
Shaun Booth (9)	107
Daniel Rowland (11)	108
Liam Shannon (9)	108
Kieran Lee (7)	109
Daniel Pridding (8)	109
Anne-Marie Holmes (10)	110
Chloe Smith (10) & Louise Edwards (11)	111
Damon Hale & Craig Bradley (10)	112
Leah Jordan (10)	113
Samuel Richardson (10)	114
Reece Tittensor & Nathan Oldham (10)	114
Jessica Husband (10)	115
Jade Leah Scrivner (9)	115
Abigail Surridge (9)	116
Jack Steed (10)	117
Alannah Stockton (11)	118
Jessica Murphy (9)	118
Adam Atherton (11)	119
Katie Pridding (11)	119
Kyle Lowe (7)	120

Craig Taylor (10)	120
Jessica Hyde (11)	121
Holly Prescott (11)	121
Chloe Statham (11)	122
Rowanne Smalley (10)	122
Georgia Knott (10)	123
Michael Redman-Johnson (11)	123
Aiden Smalley (9)	124
Toni Flynn (11)	125
Doha Salem (7)	126
Jennifer Madeley (10)	126
Samuel Swinburn (7)	127
Jake Moroney (10)	127
Elliot Jones (8)	128
Keely Maher (10)	128
Aron Bardsley (9)	129
Rebecca Myerscough (9)	129
Jakob Hitchen (9)	130
Sean Bradley (9)	130
Blake Marley & Olivia Sutcliffe (10)	131
Amy Ainsworth (9)	131
Michael Tighe (9)	132
Lauren Campbell (9)	132
Claire Wingfield (9)	133
Matthew Winstanley (10)	133
Chloe Woodcock (10)	134
Danielle Whitehead (8)	135
Rachel Hughes (8)	136
Danielle Maguire (8)	136
Jordan Lee Scattergood (9)	137
Chris Marsden (9)	137
Victoria Boardman (8)	138
Amy Parkinson (9)	138
Holly Fox (9)	139
Sarah Yates (10)	139
Tessa Herrington (10)	140
Kelsea Mullen (10)	140
Sophie Morris (11)	141
Ben Burslam (10)	141
Harry Blackwell (8)	142
Bethany Waite (8)	142
Bethany Parry (8)	143

Moorside Primary School
Ben Ashmore (8)	143
Victoria Shaw (9)	144
Kacie Andrew (7)	144
Rachel Parkinson (8)	144
Nathan Gee (8)	145
Charlotte Carr (9)	145
Kerrianne Maloney (9)	146
Dylan Yates (9)	146
Holly Jones (8)	147
Leanne Marie Sandbach (9)	147
Samantha Clarke (9)	148
Daniel Pitman (9)	148
Jessica Phillips (9)	148
Zachary M A Smith (9)	149
Chris Kinsey (9)	149
Charlotte Orton (9)	149
Sophie Woods (9)	150
Rebecca Ellis (8)	150
Thomas Pratt (8)	150
Thomas Bullock (9)	151
Cameron Conley (8)	151
Jodie Holden (8)	152
Jack Henshaw (8)	152
Chelsie O'Keeffe (9)	153
April Stanhope (8)	153
Hannah Starkie (8)	153

Rolls Crescent Primary School
Letifah Dervan (10)	154

St Mary's CE Primary School, Davyhulme
Lauren Grimshaw (9)	154
Shelby Reavy (10)	155
Amy Hall (8)	155
Joe Cooper (10)	156
Emily Hall (8)	156
Alicia McGrath (9)	157
Sam Robertshaw (7)	157
Alex Platt (10)	158
Lucy Pickering (9)	158

Martin Wood (8)	159
Oliver Rothwell (8)	159
Sarah Marland (10)	160
James Wilson-Jevon (8)	160
Jessica Walker (9)	161
Alicia Buckley (7)	161
Sophie Irving (9)	162
Luke May (8)	162
Koel Raychaudhuri (8)	163
Matthew Marshall (7)	163
Amelia Scott-Steele (9)	164
Lorna Riley (7)	164
Joe Murphy (9)	165
Sam Gilmour (8)	165
Jordan Southern (9)	166
Luke Woolstencroft (9)	166
Eleanor Wright (7)	167
Courtney Edge (9)	168
Thomas Radcliffe (10)	169
Alex Jones (9)	170
Rebecca Simister (9)	171
Helen Lyons (10)	172
Peter Dawson (9)	173
Rhea Leslie (8)	174

St Thomas More RC Primary School, Middleton

Liam Magrath (8)	174
Laura Hankinson (8)	175
Jordan Lazenbury (8)	175
Harley McIntosh (8)	176
Rhiannon Prestage (8)	176
Chloe Cripps (8)	177
Jessica Newton (8)	177
Elizabeth Stockton (8)	178
Victoria Philbin (8)	178
Jake Curran-Pipe (8)	179
Hannah Morson (10)	179
Charlotte Stockton (8)	180
Clare Rusk (9)	180
Phillip Burke (10)	181
Joachim Miller (10)	181

Stephanie Lyons (9)	182
Jonathan Mulligan (9)	182
Matthew Whittaker (10)	182
Jasmine Davies (9)	183
Olivia Coghlan (10)	183
Mitchell Cain (9)	184
Harris Faulkner (10)	184
Victoria Waters (10)	185
Stephen Maryniak (10)	185
Sophie Carey (10)	185
Lucy Rhodes (9)	186
Mason Matlock (10)	186
Sean Bamforth (8)	187
Bria Sagar (10)	187
Adam Bowler (10)	187
Joseph Beaumont (9)	188
Matthew Hayes (9)	188
Katie Carey (10)	189
Andrew Murray (9)	189
Chloe Vergine (10)	189
David Murray (9)	190
Hannah Hayes (10)	190
Peter Busby (9)	190
James Candlin (10)	191
Lois Cassin (8)	191
Benedict Miller (8)	192
Christian Walters (10)	192
Joseph Craven (10)	192

Stansfield Road Junior School

Stephanie Caldecott (9)	193
Jordan Proctor (9)	193
Alex Davison (8)	194
Jonathan Sharrock (8)	194
Sophie Brooks (8)	195
Chelsea Seale (8)	195
Olivia Willoughby (8)	196
Liam Paull (8)	196
Jamie Wetton (8)	196
Thomas Warburton (9)	197
Kayley Leasley (8)	197

Amy Grogan (8)	198
Megan Ashton (8)	198
Laura Cotterill (9)	199
Kelly-Anne Western (8)	199
Rebecca Lear (8)	200
Stephanie Macpherson (8)	200
Curtis Newton (8)	201
Savannah Dean (9)	201
Sam James (9)	202
Daniel Merrington (9)	202
Emma Lowe (9)	203
Shannon Lewis (9)	203
Charlotte Ingham (8)	204
Jenny Britain	204
Victoria Aldred (8)	205
Jordan Oliver (8)	205
Jack Bromley (8)	206

The Poems

The Boy Who Cried Wolf!

Once upon a faraway hill,
There sat a boy whose name was Bill
Bill was thinking about what he could do,
He thought and thought, a wolf came to mind.

'Wolf, Wolf!' cried the boy,
Everyone came running to the boy.
He laughed and laughed and said, 'Goodbye.'
Everyone said, 'Oh silly Bill.'

An hour later, he said again,
'Wolf,' cried the boy, 'I'm in pain.'
Everyone said, 'Oh not again,
He plays a stupid trick.'

In an hour's time he went to sleep,
A wolf came near for something to eat.
The boy woke up, saw the wolf and cried 'Wolf!'
And everyone ignored him and he died.

Susan Maria-Dawn Wood (9)
Alma Park Primary School

Love Poem

Love is as sweet as a strawberry
Love smells like roses in the air
Love is like an arrow shooting through the sky
Love is like a sigh of beauty
Love smells like tulips
Love is like beautiful flowers in the gardens
Love smells like a beautiful sweet cake
Love is like stars flying around you
Love is like fireworks speeding into the air
Love is like seeing roses everywhere.

Caseem Parveen (9)
Alma Park Primary School

Traffic Light

Sun
Bright
Shine
Bud
Colourful
Hat
Red
Green
Yellow

Dazzling
Beautiful
Powerful
Blast
Scary
Electric
Red

Powerful
Blast
Blinding
Loud
Colourful
Hot
Red
Green
Yellow

Sarah Coppersthwaite
Alma Park Primary School

Dragon

Its fire is as hot as lava
Burns prey to dust
Fierce, terrifying,
Breathes fire.

James Samuel Walker (8)
Alma Park Primary School

Love Is . . .

Love is a heart of gold
Love is playing together
Love is caring for each other
Love is a red rose.

Love is two people in love
Love is talking together
Love is a bag of friends
Love is being kind

Love is sharing ideas
Love is talking about each other
Love is trying to be helpful
Love is a sweet kiss

Love is making mistakes
Love is meeting each other
Love is giving people valentines
Love is romantic.

Kyle Paul Seddon (8)
Alma Park Primary School

My Grandmother

My grandmother
most likes to
see me
in the garden.

My grandmother
loves to play
with me.

She dreads it
when I shout out.

She hopes
for a good
and nice life.

Sayma Shaheen (9)
Alma Park Primary School

The England Beast

This monster wanders around and never sleeps
If you see him he'll give you the creeps
If you see right into his face
You'll wish you had been born in outer space.

This monster grows as fast as yeast
This monster is called the 'England Beast'
He wanders around at night
But this monster is afraid of light.

He looks like mouldy old cheese
His eyes look like dried up peas
He smells like old blood
He leaves footprints covered with mud.

C J Hammett (8)
Alma Park Primary School

Grandma

My grandma likes to see her granddaughters every Friday.
My grandma loves to play games.
My grandma dreads it when we cry.
My grandma hopes to win the lottery.
My grandma dislikes her granddaughters swearing.

Kimberley France (9)
Alma Park Primary School

Cow

Big, soft, cuddly.
Slow cow eating the green grass.
Leaping in the black mud.
It makes me feel happy.
As loud as *music*.
Spotty cow!

Rebecca Wrench (8)
Alma Park Primary School

School

Children very nervous,
Meeting all their friends.
Writing all their letters,
With their new school pens.
They're all in the playground,
Happy as can be,
Playing on the swings with a one, two, three.
When the school bell rings,
The children go to class.
Looking out the windows,
Which are made of glass.

Chelsea Rhiann Marley (9)
Alma Park Primary School

Bravery

Bravery is going to war as a knight.
Bravery is going into a house full of flames and saving a body.
Bravery is running down the road and saving a boy
Or an old lady from getting run over.
Bravery is helping your people.
Bravery is a very good thing.
Always be brave.

Mohammed Abbas (9)
Alma Park Primary School

About My Grandad

My grandad likes football.
My grandad likes chunky popcorn.
My grandad loves to watch cricket.
My grandad loves to win the lottery.
My grandad loves to say, 'Happy anniversary!'
My grandad loves to sit down and read the paper.

Jake Paton (10)
Alma Park Primary School

At The Football Match

I hear the people's songs as they echo,
The blue surrounds me, screaming *'Goal!'*
And further down I've been told,
Of a football and a cup of gold,
At the football, at the football match!

There are swarms and swarms of replica shirts,
Their favourite players covered in dirt,
The goalkeepers and players seem to be hurt,
At certain times they produce an energy spurt,
At the football, at the football match!

The blues 2, the reds 0, the game's only at halftime
                                    and seems to be won,
But obviously we're not done,
As the players descend to the dressing room,
At the football, at the football match!

Bang, smack! The ball's in the net,
'2-1,' I scream, 'it's not over yet.'
A 3-1 win was my bet,
And I'm ripping up when I've got a debt,
From North Manchester police and Miss Jones' vet,
At the football, at the football match.

The game is over, I howl, 'I'm rich!'
And then, drunk, I fall crash in a ditch!
My story has one little glitch
Anelka crashed down on the football pitch
At the football, at the football match

Now wait because here is the catch
It's the end of the football match.

Tom Patrick Cragg Bishop (10)
Alma Park Primary School

Love Is . . .

Love is happiness.
Love is like a friend.
Love is like taking a person to a park.
Love is like being jolly.
Love is like a hug.
Love is like a party.
Love is like a kiss.
Love is like having a beer.

Laveeza Waseem (8)
Alma Park Primary School

Eagles

Eagles are flying and gliding through the air,
Fast, huge, gliding.
Makes me feel like I am their next meal!
Gliding in the air ever so fast after their prey.
Eyesight like a deadly robot.
As fast as the speed of light.
Eagles are dancing in the air.
    Gliding and soaring in the air.
    Fast eagle.

Asim Saeed (9)
Alma Park Primary School

Cat

Black, silly, slim.

A sly cat catches a bird.
A cat creeps into the house.
It makes me feel like a spring flower, light and fresh.
As light as the breeze.

    Soft cat.

Harriet Jessica Mann (8)
Alma Park Primary School

Ian

He likes to swim
with me and race me.

He loves to see me happy,
also having fun.

He dreads to see me
arguing over him.

He hopes to see me
again with my sister.

He dislikes my sister
being horrible over him to me.

Jade Appleyard (10)
Alma Park Primary School

The Explorer's Attic

Didgeridoos covered in dust,
and pale brown Aboriginal masks,
and wigwams that are broken down.

The drips are loud in the immense silence,
cockroaches running and scuttling over my feet,
and the spirits are howling and haunting.

A rancid stink,
spreading in the attic,
a sour smell getting worse and worse.

The cockroaches crunching under my feet,
the dust in the form of a million specks,
The rigid edges of the broken tiles.
Where has he been?

Daniel Watts (8)
Button Lane School

Lightning

As the lightning strikes,
and the thunder stomps,
it is as if there are cannon and gunshots
echoing as night is no more.
As the clouds become dark,
the sound of thunder and the sight of lightning
travel across the land.
The lightning flashes in the twilight sky,
illuminating any object in its path.
The dark stormy clouds roll across the wide open sky.
The thunder's groan echoes again and again.
As the volume rises it's like the war is rising
from the jaws of Hell.
Suddenly the clouds burst and down comes the rain.
The wind crashes around my face.
The wind and rain create a face.
It is as if they have been combined into one.
When the darkness fades away, the moon disappears
and out comes the bright sun.

Mark Hudson (10)
Button Lane School

A Seagull

A seagull's cry is like a seal stuck under a rock, desperate
                                                             to be freed.
The seagull's wings flap as if an engine is trying to start.
They swoop down from the sky like a plane falling from the air.

The waves rush between my toes as I walk barefoot along the beach.
Tiny grains of sand stick to my ankles and feet like glue.
Shingle crackles as the waves push and pull along the shoreline.
I listen carefully as the sea animals make strange sounds.

Steven Dodd (10)
Button Lane School

The Late-Night Princess

The glistening sun settles down,
The princess is awake,
Wearing a diamond tiara and a flowing gown.

The princess is sweetly singing
The bulby bells are ringing
The children are asleep

Bumpy fairy wings
And soft wavy hair
And the beautiful silk-covered throne

Spongy fairy cakes that melt in the mouth
Fizzy purple lemon drink
And edible fairy dust that falls from the sky.

Sweet-smelling lavenders
Berry bluebells
And the smell of apple pie all through the house.

She has a secret of her own, but we know, don't we?

Soraya Chiheb (9)
Button Lane School

Thunder And Lightning

Thunder crashing is like a fierce battle,
Cannons blasting,
Never-ending.
The lightning banging sounds like a sniper shooting,
Men down,
Soldiers screaming,
Blood is pouring,
The wind blows trees down,
Cars tip over,
Stones tumble down the road and block the grids.
Windows crash and smash,
People fall to the ground.

Leon Potter (10)
Button Lane School

Wild Weather

The thunder is like hundreds
of guns flying in the sky.
Bang, blast, boom.
The rain is like a child
playing in the pool
Splash, splosh, spatter.
The lightning is like a torch
slashing in the darkness
Flash, spark, twinkle.
The hailstones are like stones
dropping from the sky
Tapping, tapping.
Snowflakes are like white gems
falling out of the clouds
falling silently on the ground.
The tornado is like a hairdryer
The wind and noise
Roaring, howling, whistling.
The sun is like a warm and hot bed
Fiery, scorching, boiling.
A hurricane is like an enormous fan
Crashing, banging, rolling!

Kelly West (11)
Button Lane School

Nature

The sun is an orange football illuminating the world.
The sky is like a blue carpet dotted with blobs of marshmallow.
The moon is a bright light that shines in the sky.
The sea is like a flood that has soaked the world.
The stars are like glitter shining in the distance.
Rain is like a leak in the sky.
The grains of sand sparkle through the gaps in my hand.
The grass is as green as an emerald reflecting beauty into my eyes.

Andrew Chappell (11)
Button Lane School

The Explorer's Attic

Dusty old treasures.
Crooked bent photos.
Torn papyrus.
He's been everywhere.

Rats scuttling around.
Blue crunchy cockroaches.
Wind howling rapidly.
What a disturbing place.

Rotten dust jumping from cobweb to cobweb.
Black torn-up sprouts.
Dripping water from the rusty pipes.
It's very smelly.

The dusty air blowing.
Mouldy fruit burning…
Rust, sand spilling.
This tastes horrid.

Spongy soft cobwebs.
Silky rusty dust.
The squashed cockroaches.
What a mess!

Aimee Price (9)
Button Lane School

The Light

The dancing flames are colourful in the open grate.
Light sparkles in the midnight-black sky.
It's blinding white in the cloudless evening.
It's blood-red in a lamp.
It is orange like glowing street lamps.
It sparkles white-hot on the end of a firework.
It reflects off a gleaming car windscreen.
Starlight reflects off the full moon.
Light is extremely magical.

Natalie Sheridan (11)
Button Lane School

I Had A Dream Last Night

I had a dream last night
I had a dream last night
I had a dream last night
When the sky was blue
When the sky was blue
When the sky was blue
It was a really good dream
It was a really good dream
It was a really good dream
It was about a wand
It was about a wand
It was about a wand
The wand put on a spell
The wand put on a spell
The wand put on a spell
The spell was snapped
The spell was snapped
The spell was snapped
The wand cried
The wand cried
The wand cried
The wand died
The wand died
The wand died.

Alex Herd (7)
Button Lane School

Colourful Colours

Red is the colour of roses.
Blue is the colour of violets.
Green is the colour of leaves.
Yellow is the colour of dandelions.
Purple is the colour of tulips.
Dark green is the colour of trees.
White is the colour of lilies.

Ryan Gillman (7)
Button Lane School

The Seaside

The seagulls cry as loud as owls howling
the stones as smooth as melting chocolate
the seagulls are as white as snow
the crowd is in chaos and as loud as can be

The leaves are as green as grass
the sea is as blue as my jumper
and as soft as my book
the trees are as tall as Blackpool Tower
reaching to the sky

The daisies smell really fresh
the tree branches are as hard as rock
the sun is like a tangerine
the fantasy of a day at Blackpool
is what this means to me

The shells are as small as can be.
Oh what can I see?
Oh what can I see?

The sun is as bright
as a light bulb shining in my eye
the sea is lovely
the ducks are quacking
'Danger, stay away!'

Laura Jane Fielding (11)
Button Lane School

Thunder Is . . .

Thunder is like a rocket blasting into space,
Thunder is like a cannon firing in the war,
Thunder is like a car engine backfiring,
Thunder is like a scratching noise,
Thunder is like a cheering crowd,
Thunder is like a banging drum.

Nick Morrow (11)
Button Lane School

The Witches' Kitchen

Witches cackle
Bats rattle
Bubbling cauldron, *cackle, cackle.*
Bones crunching
Eyes looking
Slime slithering
Oh, what a horrible place!
Dusty spells
Slimy elves
Dotty shelves
Witches licking liver
Spiders' legs quiver
They're all revolting!

Sophie Anne Dalton (8)
Button Lane School

Light, Light

Light, light, so colourful and bright,
In the morning, afternoon, day and night.
Light, light, how you glow and spark,
Helping us to see in light and dark.
Light, light, how you shimmer and shine,
Helping us to see from line to line.
Light, light, you go and come,
Turn off my light and watch the setting sun.
Light, light, everywhere,
Watching you, and how you dance and flare.

Jessica Yiu (11)
Button Lane School

The Witch's Kitchen

Cauldron lies old and dusty.
Slimy and brainy eyeball.
Black sticky bugs.

Footsteps plodding.
The spirits creaking.
Large black spiders biting.

Horrid cheeses.
The witch's smelly feet.
Sticky mould on the shelves.

Slime sticking on walls.
Rock-hard bread with spiderwebs.
In the witch's horrible kitchen.

Megan Barnes (9)
Button Lane School

The Weather

The thunderstorm illuminates the midnight sky.
Forks of lightning stab the blanket of stars.
Cracks of thunder and splashes of light
remind me of the war and I feel like I want to cry.
The wind crashes around my face.
The hailstones are like a beating drum
echoing through the night.
As they hit the ground, the world appears to turn white.

Mohammad Jaberansari (11)
Button Lane School

The Call Of Weather

The fluffy clouds are like marshmallow
swaying from side to side.
Some are like bunny rabbits rolling
across the blue carpet.
Snowflakes are like tears which have frozen.
The rain trickles between my fingers
and runs down my face.
As the drops fall to the ground
I hear *pitter-patter ping!*

The thunder is like a million gunshots.
Bang! Boom! Crash!

Chloe Potter (10)
Button Lane School

What Am I?

I creep through the jungle,
Spying on my prey, as quiet as a mouse,
But then . . . as quick as a flash,
My claws come out to play,
Slash, slash, slash, slash, as quick as a flash!
The prey falls to the ground,
I will beat you at anything,
Beat ya, beat ya,
What am I?

Answer - a cheetah!

Anthony Stone (11)
Button Lane School

The Weather Poem

A thunderstorm is like a thousand cannons
in World War I
The claps of thunder remind me of two cars
colliding on a slippery road.
My face is drenched with gallons of water
sliding down my cheeks.
The sparks of lightning remind me of a
warm crackling fire.

The rain is like the seagulls pecking at
the windowpanes.
As the rain subsides, the road gets drier and drier.
The world feels fresh after the storm has gone.

Rebekah Layfield-Cole (10)
Button Lane School

The Alien Spacecraft

The alien dripping with blood.
The head was off when they were walking.
They were leaving a trail of blood.

People screaming for help.
People were killing more.
They were flying around in the spinning metal saucer.

You could smell the alien skin.
Rotten milk, burnt bread.
It stung my nostrils.

Andrew Stewart (9)
Button Lane School

My Dog

My dog is white, beautiful and pretty
She has brown eyes.
She has flippy floppy ears.
She has a long, long, white tail.
She has not got any spots on her.
She runs really fast.
She waggles her tail.
She even catches the cat.
I love her to bits!
She flicks her mouth as she drinks.
She smells her food as it goes into the bowl.

Bethany Miller (8)
Button Lane School

School Is Boring

I hate school.
I hate school.
It is so boring but we have to go to school.
I don't want to go because it is boring.
We don't get to play but the teachers get to drink tea.
It is not fair.
I've got a new teacher
She is called Ms Phillips.
She is kind.
I love school!

Ellé Bates (7)
Button Lane School

The Storm

Lightning crackles like a witch's evil laugh,
As the pouring rain trickles down my back,
The murky, slate-grey clouds float all about,
People around me are scared and they scream and shout,
With frowns on their faces and their hats blowing away,
People in houses bend down and pray,
For the frightening thunder and the cold climatic rain,
After this terrible storm, nothing will be the same again,
Stop, please storm, just let us be,
And don't come back again for eternity,
The children inside are running around,
But the people who were outside cannot be found!

Amy Smith (10)
Button Lane School

Spooky Castle

Creaking floorboards
Someone's coming
Or is it my imagination . . . ?

Smell of burnt toast
Awful sour milk
A rattle like fish bones

The lights flick on
Slimy spiders
Wriggling, jiggling on the floorboards.

Jessica Lee (9)
Button Lane School

Enrique The Cat

We got a cat at Xmas
He's black from head to toe
He eats his food so fast
But then he runs quite slow.

We finally called him Enrique
A friend for our hamster, Patch
He really likes to jump and play
But he can give you a scratch.

The cat's now used to us all
When you stroke him he gives you a purr
He dashes and runs for his ball
There's no scratch in his lovely, black fur.

James Fisher (8)
Chorlton CE Primary School

Koala

A fluffy feature that lives in the jungle.
An animal that clings to trees.
A tiny mammal that eats leaves.
A creature that looks like a scary dog.
A creature that sits on a log.
A tiny animal with big claws.
A marsupial that carries babies.
A jungle-liver

Who am I?

Answer - A koala!

Karla Murphy (10)
Chorlton CE Primary School

Weird And Wonderful Food

Apples are atomic for artful ants.
Bananas are bizarre for bossy bulls.
Colgate is cleansing for crazy cats.
Doughnuts are delicious for delighted daddies.
Eggs are an example for excellent elephants.
Fish are fast for fabulous fairies.
Grapes are great for ginormous gorillas.
Ham is horrific for horrid hogs.
Ice cream is interesting for interpreting ibex.
Jam is juicy for jealous jellyfish.
Kiwis are kicking for kind koalas.
Lettuce is lovely for long lizards.
Marzipan is marvellous for munching mummies.
Nuts are nervous for noisy nurses.
Oats are open for out-sized ostriches.
Pineapples are precious for preaching parrots.
Quinces are quick for quicker quails.
Runner beans are realistic for running rabbits.
Sausages are saucy for soft snakes.
Toast is testing for touchy teachers.
Upside down cakes are uppermost for 'hungry 'umans.
Violet creams are vibrant for vivacious vixens.
Watermelons are wet for watching wallabies.
Xtra strong mints are xtra hot
Yolks are yummy for yapping yaks.
Zuchini is zooming for zesty zebras.

Rebecca Barber (10)
Chorlton CE Primary School

Dragon Cinquain

Dragon
A burning flame
Dangerous with its claws
Eyes sparkle like an emerald
Dragon.

Nathan Dalby (11)
Chorlton CE Primary School

Snow Time

Snow is falling, falling to the ground,
Girls and boys running around.
The snow as white as icing sugar,
Surely it can't be summer?

In the country a blanket covers the land,
No need for hot, sunny sand.
Sledging down those snowy hills,
What's the point for winter blues?

You're fast asleep in your bed,
And this is what Jack Frost said,
'I'll make the snow and ice appear,
I'll make them tremble with fear!'

Now the snow has nearly gone,
New lambs and flowers are sprung upon.
The sunny days are nearly here,
Oh well, there's snow again next year.

Lauren Newbery (10)
Chorlton CE Primary School

My Brother

My brother sits and watches a cartoon,
While I clean up his room.
My brother hurts himself on a game,
And I get the blame.
It's time to go out,
'Do I have to?' I shout.
My mum buys him a toy,
She says it's because he's a boy.
The next place we stop,
Is at a clothes shop.
My mum buys me the dress of my dreams,
While my brother stands and screams.

Bethan Ward (8)
Chorlton CE Primary School

Who Am I?

Always caring
Helps you sharing
Never hates
Super and great
Cooks for you
Makes money too
My best mate
Drives me to school so I'm never late
Made of love
Gives me hugs
Never gives frowns
Doesn't make silly sounds
She is the best
Smartly dressed
She is so clever
There is nobody better

Who am I?

Answer - My mum.

Tom Byrne (10)
Chorlton CE Primary School

Alliteration Poem

Burgers are beautiful for batty beasts
Carrots are cool for cheeky chimps
Donuts are delicious for dotty ducks
Eggs are excellent for excited elephants
Fries are fantastic for fabulous frogs
Grapes are gorgeous for grand giraffes
Ham is handy for hungry hippos
Ice is interesting for incapable iguanas
Jam is justified for jolly jaguars
KitKats are kinder for kicking kangaroos
Lemons are lively for leaping lions.

Connor Turner (9)
Chorlton CE Primary School

The Ghost House

It creeps in the dark,
Jumps out to scare,
People in the ghost house, do beware!

It makes the stairs creak,
Turns your blood into ice,
It really isn't very nice!

Hovering about,
Making you scream,
Surely, this is just a dream?

It takes you by surprise,
Scares you out of your wits,
You wonder, 'What is it?'

You take a look,
You're in for a shock,
You're in a room, it turns the lock!

You're really scared,
In a room with a ghost,
The thing that you hate most . . .

Argh!

Kenneth Chung (9)
Chorlton CE Primary School

My Shoes

My shoes, my shoes, big and small,
Flat and wide but that's not all.
Some are black, some are blue,
Some are silver for that special 'do'.

I'm always asking for new shoes,
It really helps me beat the blues.

They make me feel bright and breezy,
Keeping me happy is really easy.

Hannah Miller (10)
Chorlton CE Primary School

Bullies

I went to school today,
But I didn't want to.

I went to school today,
Wondering what to do.

I went to school today,
Knowing that the bullies
Would be there.

I went to school today,
For me, no one cared.

I went to school today,
Why can't they leave me be?

I went to school today,
The bullies were after me.

Louisa Cole (11)
Chorlton CE Primary School

Yummy Food

Carrots are cool for colourful cats.
Burgers are beautiful for batty beasts.
Pizzas are peckish for panicky penguins.
Cakes are crunchy for cowardly caterpillars.
Ice creams are icy for independent intellectuals.
Puddings are perfect for purple pelicans.
Sandwiches are scrumptious for silly snakes.
Apples are adorable for anxious astronauts.
Grapes are great for giant gardeners.
Toasts are terrific for terrifying tortoises.
Yoghurts are yummy for yawning yetis.
Strawberries are stupid for starving slugs.
Pineapples are prickly for personal pandas.
Hollies are happy for hearty humans.
Eggs are enthusiastic for enormous elephants.
Winders are watery for weird women.

Saqib Ashraf (9)
Chorlton CE Primary School

Winter Wonder World

A blizzard blew and covered the land
like a ghostly galleon being tossed around.

The ice covered the land with frost
but still all signs of warmth were lost.

Vanilla ice cream was seen once more
as the snow fell like never before.

'It's gone, it's gone, it such a shame.'
'What's gone?'

Winter is its name!

Chelise-Ray Davies (10)
Chorlton CE Primary School

Food

Food, food, I love to eat.
Vegetables, fruit, sweets and meat.

I like all foods except tuna and cheese,
Eggs are horrid, I don't like these.

Chips and pizza make me happy,
They are yummy and fill my tummy.

Emma Clare (8)
Chorlton CE Primary School

A Motorbike

You switch a button on
You kick it to start
You pull a clutch back
With a race in your heart
You put it into first gear
And let the clutch go.

Callum Bird (11)
Chorlton CE Primary School

Kenning

A sneaky stalker
A prey warper
A bush shaker
A cub waker
A night-time eater
A daytime meeter
An animal preyer
An antelope slayer

What am I?

Answer - A tiger.

Amy Heathcote (10)
Chorlton CE Primary School

The Deer

The deer has antlers like a plant.
He opens free to nature.
If he gets into a fight he stops
And dashes away
Into the swirling, whirling jungle.
While darting away from his foe
He vanishes into the green shadows.

Matthew Charles Edwards (8)
Chorlton CE Primary School

My Dad's Singing

Have you heard my dad sing?
When he warbles
He breaks every bauble
We tell him to stop,
But then the windows go
Pop!

Danny Vose (10)
Chorlton CE Primary School

A Joey

A high jumper
A milk sucker
A pouch hider
A desert strider
A clumsy boxer
A prince of the Aussie world
A size twelve footer
An Aussie creature

Who am I?

Answer - A joey

Rory Jack McGagh (10)
Chorlton CE Primary School

Animals Over For Tea

Carrots are cool for cunning cats.
Ham is heavy for hungry hamsters.
Tuna is tasty for ticklish turtles.
Pizza is perfect for peckish penguins.
Burgers are brilliant for beautiful butterflies.
Seaweed is super for swimming sharks.
Every kind of food is excellent for every kind of animal.

Laurie Emma Micallef (10)
Chorlton CE Primary School

What Is For What?

Leeks are lovely for laughing lions.
Bananas are brilliant for bouncing baboons.
Apples are awesome for angry ants.
Cabbage is cunning for cruel cats.
Salad is sick for singing snails.
Tomato is tough for tiny teachers.

Oskar Sutton (9)
Chorlton CE Primary School

Teachers

T eachers are people, who come from college,
E asily remembering not to go insane,
A nd memorising the children safety rule,
C losing their 'Beginner's Teacher's Handbook'
H astily thinking how horrible the kids might be,
E ating their lunch whilst discussing their new schools,
R ealising how complicated kids always are!
S uddenly they regret doing their teaching exam!

Adil Danyal Anwar (9)
Chorlton CE Primary School

A Golden Buttercup

In my hand I hold
a buttercup of gold.
A brave and shining fellow
in his coat of yellow.
With his golden eye
he stares into the big, blue sky
and nods his rounded head
wherever children tread.

Isabella Rees (8)
Chorlton CE Primary School

Football

F ouls are foolish for fabulous footballers
O wn goals are obliging for opposing opponents
O ffside is OK on obvious occasions
T ime is ticking for tense tactics
B irmingham's Bennet blocks the ball
A ssitants attend to aggressive attackers
L iverpool's Lee likes lobbing
L ights are lit for luminous lobs.

Dilan Mohiedin (9)
Chorlton CE Primary School

My Perfect Holiday

Going on holiday
to sunny Spain,
on the beach
where you can't get rain.
Swimming in the Mediterranean Sea,
out to a restaurant
my family and me.

Licking ice creams in the sun,
playing ball,
it's so much fun.
Reading my book
on the sand,
it's so exciting,
trembling in my hand.

Florence Millar (9)
Chorlton CE Primary School

The Alpha Animals

Bananas are beautiful for batty bats
Crisps are cool for crazy cats
Grapes are gorgeous for grizzly gorillas
Ham is hilarious for hiking hares
Melons are mighty for mini mice
Pasta is peculiar for pecking penguins
Rice is real for rapid rats
Salad is supreme for silly seals
Tuna is ticklish for tanned tigers
Lime is lovely for lively lambs
Ice cream is ideal for itchy iguanas
Eggs are excellent for enormous elephants.

Stavros Sapountzis (10)
Chorlton CE Primary School

Introducing The A To Z Family

A unty Able answers accurately,
B eautiful Bertha beams bashfully,
C areful Catherine canters cautiously,
D aft David doodles deliberately,
E normous Eric enters erratically,
F amous Fred follows freely,
G ardener Gary grows grapes gratefully,
H omely Harry helps happily,
I ndependent Ivy imitates instantly,
J umping James juggles jokingly,
K ing Karl kisses kindly,
L oopy Lu laughs loudly,
M enacing Mabel messes merrily,
N eat Nina nurses nimbly,
'O rrible Otis 'obbles oddly,
P odgy Peter pursues patiently,
Q uirky Quentin quivers quickly,
R ansom Raymond rules rudely,
S imple Simon stares strangely,
T errible Tara tears ties tamely,
U nderstanding Ursula undresses untidily,
V ampire Vera vacuums viciously,
W eird William washes windows wonderfully,
'X citing Xena xylophones 'xcellently,
Y ing Yong yells yearningly,
Z any Zara zooms zealously,
   And that is the whole of the A to Z family.

Talia Ogunyemi (10)
Chorlton CE Primary School

The Owl And The Dog
(In The Style of Edward Lear)

The owl and the dog went to the moon,
On a sparkling, silver spoon,
They took some tins and plenty of pins,
Wrapped up on a big, brown broom,
They never forgot their dogs,
Susie and Socks,
One had chickenpox,
And the other as hard as rocks,
They both liked to bark,
'Woof, woof.'
'Woof, woof.'
They both liked to bark.
'Woof woof.'
The owl said, 'This moon is hot,
I wonder what we can do,
Let's look for a teapot before we get shot,
We get shot,
We get shot,
Before we get shot,' he said.
They found a teapot and hid inside,
He said, 'It's a good job it's wide
It's wide,
It's wide,
It's a good job it's wide.'

Demi-Lea Fraine (10)
Church of England School of The Resurrection

My Sisters

They are the most precious diamonds,
They are huge coloured rainbows,
They are the biggest smile on my face,
And they are my glowing light
In complete darkness; they are my sisters.

Abbie Sherwin (9)
Church of England School of The Resurrection

Petrified

When I was eight,
I went on a ride.
And when I got on,
I was petrified.

The ride went up,
The ride went down.
When it started,
It twirled me around.

The ride wouldn't stop,
So I shouted my mum.
She told the man,
And it stopped near the sun.

I went on another ride,
And it went slow.
I waved to my mum,
As it started to go.

Tasha Dodd (9)
Church of England School of The Resurrection

Weather

The sky lights up with a bolt of lightning,
Children think it is very frightening,
Like a firework in the sky,
The light and noise makes them cry.

A big roar, a clap of thunder
Such light, such noise, it makes you wonder
Is it God's anger or just a storm?
I prefer summer, it is nice and warm.

Hanna Delaney (9)
Church of England School of The Resurrection

10th Birthday

When it's your 10th birthday,
You turn a big one 0.
My mate asked if I was having a party,
I said, 'Gosh, I don't know.'

So I went home wondering,
If I was going to have one,
I went into my living room,
But everyone had gone.

So I went into the kitchen,
I couldn't believe my eyes,
Because my family,
Had left me a big surprise!

Ashley Mottram (10)
Church of England School of The Resurrection

What If . . .

What if my bed turned into a jet?
This is what I would expect,
I would fly and fly in the deep blue sky
And I would wave goodbye . . .

As I flew over the deep blue sea,
I hummed a song in harmony.
I landed in a strange town,
Where people were walking upside down.

Next I found a sunny beach,
And I bought a drink with the flavour of peach.
I flew my bed back to my house,
I fell asleep as quiet as a mouse.

Kemi Awodiji (10)
Church of England School of The Resurrection

The Sun And The Moon

The sun and the moon sang a tune up high in the sky,
They stayed in Heaven until they were seven,
Were seven,
Were seven,
They stayed in Heaven until they were seven,
They were going to get married,
In a beautiful green carriage,
They wrapped up some jars and plenty of stars,
For their long journey,
They travelled on a sun called Burney,
Burney,
Burney,
They travelled on a sun called Burney.

Lauren Nagle-Moth (10)
Church of England School of The Resurrection

James Bond And Harry Potter

Harry and James got into the Aston Martin DB5,
And drove to MI6's base,
They took two cars,
And plenty of gadgets in brown suitcases,
James said, 'Let's make haste.'
But Harry was making a potions paste.
Harry had finished,
James had a taste,
      Had a taste,
           Had a taste,
James had a taste.

Phillip Joseph Chatburn (!0)
Church of England School of The Resurrection

Running

I'm winning a race, I'm in first place,
I start to slow and go into second place,
I eventually get going again,
I'm winning again.
I am running and I fall over,
I am in last place,
I get up and I'm running again,
I win the race!

Patrick Souter (10)
Church of England School of The Resurrection

Humpty Dumpty

Humpty Dumpty went to the moon,
On a supersonic spoon,
He took some porridge and a tent,
But when he landed the spoon bent.
Humpty said he didn't care,
For all I know, he's still up there!

Darion Blackett (9)
Church of England School of The Resurrection

Mum And Dad

They are like guardian angels,
They bring love to my heart,
They have a job to care for me,
They are like a star floating above me,
They are my true love,
My mum and dad.

Danielle Purcell (8)
Church of England School of The Resurrection

Snow

As shiny as a crystal.
It sticks to your gloves.
It is as sticky as glue.
It is as cold as a freezer.
It feels like slush.
It melts in your hands.
You can make a snowman.
It came while I was asleep.
It is so white.
It makes me shiver.

Robyn Cannon (7)
Church of England School of The Resurrection

I Am . . .

I am like an angel floating with the wind,
I am like luxury, even in paradise,
I am like a baby, so soft and delicate,
I am like sweets falling from the sky,
I am . . . a snowflake.

Jacquelinejade Mason (9)
Church of England School of The Resurrection

I Am . . .

I am like glitter falling from the sky,
I am as delicate as a brand new ornament,
I am as fragile as a newborn baby,
If you crush me I will break like glass,
I am a snowflake.

Naomi Yong (9)
Church of England School of The Resurrection

Twinkle, Twinkle Little Cat

Twinkle, twinkle little cat,
Why do I wonder what you're at?
Looking at the mice so high,
They're like tea trays in the sky.
Watch that dog around the corner,
Otherwise you'll end up like Jack Horner.
Twinkle, twinkle little cat,
Why do I wonder what you're at?

Charlotte Palmer (8)
Church of England School of The Resurrection

Ice

The ice is cold.
It's like a crystal.
It feels like a storm pushing you.
It is cold like a freezer.
The ice covers the puddles.
Ice cools down your throat.
Ice melts when it is hot.

Kane Gardner (8)
Church of England School of The Resurrection

Incy Wincy Ant

Incy wincy ant,
Climbed up a plant,
He forgot he was small,
And had a great fall,
And we never saw him again.

Rebecca Isherwood (7)
Church of England School of The Resurrection

The Breezy Wind

As breezy as the trees
It blows you down the streets
It is windier than a breeze
As clear as water
As noisy as a Hoover
As touchy as a fire
It is a big desire
It sounds like a whistle
Whistling in the distance.

Abbie Taylor (9)
Church of England School of The Resurrection

The Wind

The wind is heavy.
The wind is cold.
The wind is like ice.
It pushes you down the street.
The wind feels like the snow.
It never goes away even when it's summer.
You can hear it but you can't see it.
You can feel it.

Chelsea Dunn Winder (8)
Church of England School of The Resurrection

Snow

Snow is like a crystal,
It is so soft,
It is as cold as ice,
And slippery and nice,
It makes your hands cold,
It crunches in your hands.

Katy Chatburn (8)
Church of England School of The Resurrection

A Snowy Night

It was a snowy night like foam
And it was cold like the sea
It was slippery like a shining floorboard
It was shiny like a crystal
It was hard like a rock
It looked like a hall of fame
It was shiny like a metal chain
That had just been bought.

Edwin Nurse (9)
Church of England School of The Resurrection

The Sun Burns The Sky

The sun burns the sky.
It dries up the puddles.
It gives you a suntan.
It makes you go red.
The sun sometimes makes you sweat,
Then sometimes keeps you awake.

Chloé Hoskison-Elliott (8)
Church of England School of The Resurrection

Jack And Jill

Jack and Jill took a pill,
And drank a glass of water.
They had such a headache,
They made the glass break,
And swept it up in the morning.

Kane O'Connor (9)
Church of England School of The Resurrection

There Was A Young Lady From France

There was a young lady from France
And she always kicked as she danced.
She danced so high and kicked so high,
She touched the sky,
And never got another chance.

Miqat Chowdhury (8)
Church of England School of The Resurrection

Friends

Friends make you laugh.
Friends make you happy.
Friends always share things.
Friends are playful.
Friends are kind.
Friends tell you jokes.
But one thing I like about my friends,
They always make me happy.
I like it when friends smile at me.

Ruqayya Ashraf (9)
Crowcroft Park Primary School

Valentine's Day

My present is ready for Valentine's Day.
I don't have to wrap it or hide it away.
I can carry it with me all day long,
It's just a smile and a happy song.
If you think it's boring you are definitely wrong.
So you'd better enjoy it, it doesn't last long.
If you can stop yourself from crying, you must be strong.
When it comes to that day, I will play with my friends,
But to buy you presents, I will use all my spends.

Tristan Schofield (10)
Crowcroft Park Primary School

Valentine's Day

V alentine's Day is on the 14th February,
A nd you need to give lots of hugs and kisses to Mum and Dad.
L ove is best on Valentine's Day.
E veryone is happy with chocolate treats.
N ow everyone is getting a card off me.
T ricks from me as I pull out the roses.
I n the party everyone tells you that they love you.
N ow the day is nearly over.
E veryone is still excited.
S o I'm jumping up and down.

D ad said, 'Thanks for a lovely day.'
A nd it was great, specially the party.
Y es, it's over now, it was wicked!

Georgina Grimshaw (9)
Crowcroft Park Primary School

Valentine's Day!

On 14th February, it's Valentine's Day.
My mum and dad buy me sweets,
You get cards, presents and flowers,
And lots of wicked treats.

On Valentine's Day I'm really excited,
My mum gives me kisses on Valentine's Day,
I tell my mum how much I love her,
I've bought her lots of presents, I say.

My little brother gave me a hair band,
The colour was red and pink,
My dad gave me a talking bear,
And when you pressed it, the noise went *clink!*

Samra Tabasum (10)
Crowcroft Park Primary School

Seasons

In spring the flowers blossom,
New animals are born,
Easter has come,
So celebrate everyone!

In summer the sun shines!
The fruits ripen,
The beaches crowd,
People eat ice cream!

In autumn the leaves fall,
The trees are stripped,
The days are short,
The sky is dull and dark.

In winter the ground is white,
The air is cold,
The spirit of Christmas has come,
And so has Santa!

Fanika Saeeda (10)
Crowcroft Park Primary School

Valentine's Day Poem

'I' is for a problem that you can't solve!
Then you see the girl of your dreams,
Then your problem's solved.

'L' is for luxury chocolates that you can get.
Chocolate is for a beauty kiss,
That you can't miss or forget.

'O' is for a decent match,
That means love is in the air,
That means you have made your match,
Now good luck from me.

Danielle Anderson (10)
Crowcroft Park Primary School

Valentine's Day

V ery kind people
A lways will love you
L ike you,
E njoy you,
N ever will hate you,
T ell you good things.
I n your spare time,
N ever eat too much chocolate,
E at sweets.
S illy people make you laugh.

D elightful people are still loving,
A nd always will be kind and giving,
Y ou can give people the love back on Valentine's Day.

Sinnika Bernard (10)
Crowcroft Park Primary School

Friends!

A friend is your very best friend,
You play games with them,
Because you know your friendship will never end,
You give gifts to them,
And they make you laugh,
They invite you home,
And they don't make any new friends,
Because you and they know,
Your friendship will,
    never,
      never,
        end!

Sana Rathore (10)
Crowcroft Park Primary School

Valentine's Day

V alentine's Day is all about love
A ll around the world people celebrate Valentine's Day
L ove is strong
E veryone needs someone to love
N obody hates anyone on Valentine's Day
T ough enough is love
I know that love is strong
N ever hate anyone on Valentine's Day
E veryone kisses someone
S o you see, love is really, really strong

D ads and mums kiss kids
A lways be kind on Valentine's Day
Y ou will know if someone loves you soon.

Ikra Ahmed (10)
Crowcroft Park Primary School

Valentine's Day

Valentine's Day is a day for romance,
You can have a party and dance,
Have you got a date?
It's not a time to hate,
Valentine's Day is very exciting,
There's a chance you'll get a ring,
If you fret for every day you go out,
Then on Valentine's Day, there should be no doubt,
Especially if you receive a red rose,
If you have no one there might be a chance he'll propose,
It will be good if you win the lottery on Valentine's Day,
You might go to Australia and lie on the bay.

Anahita Karimi (9)
Crowcroft Park Primary School

The River

As the rain
crashes down
everybody starts to
frown, as it flows from
the source, it begins its
heroic course, banging sharply
against the rocks, muddy
shoes and soggy socks as
the water hits your
feet, it is cold, it
has no heat, when it
slithers like a snake.
It gives me a huge
headache, and as the
river approaches the
sea, it calms
down and makes me
happy.

Ciaran Ryan (10)
Denton West End Primary School

The Morning The World Was White . . .

The snow was deep and covered my feet, and sparkled
Through the warm breeze,
The soft silky snow shimmered and sparkled through
The shiny light of the morning sun,
It crunched as I strode through it, and followed my path
Wherever I went,
It trickled down from the white sky,
Snowmen seemed to dance - all in different shapes and sizes,
The ice-cold snow melted through my warm gloves,
And its white blanket covered the ground.

Amy Potts (10)
Denton West End Primary School

A Bear Of Mine

My bear would be white or brown
Purple, pink, orange too!
Multicoloured is alright but
Best of all white! Yes! White!

My bear would be light,
Light as a feather,
Light as a kite,
It wouldn't weigh a hundred stones,
Because that is too heavy for me to hold.

My bear would be fluffy,
Very short fur but not too short,
Its paws would be brown, very light,
If it fell I would catch it with might.

My bear would be soft,
Its face would be white,
Its nose would be brown,
Its eyes would be black
I would buy it from town but best of all . . .
It would be mine!

Cu-Yeon Lee (9)
Denton West End Primary School

The Morning The World Was White . . .

The snow was glistening white,
As white as a polar bear.
Elegant, falling like a bird,
Cold as ice yet as soft and comfy as a warm bed.
See the snowballs fly past your head,
And the snowmen so still and unyielding.
The silky, sliding snow under your cold feet,
The snow is a blanket that covers the ground.
A winter *wonderland!*

Benjamin Lowndes (11)
Denton West End Primary School

The River

Speeding
down the
river, as it
goes so fast.
Swimming and
crashing together with one huge *blast!*
It runs like wild, be warned young child.
As it starts
very gently, suddenly
splash!
As it falls it
runs past you in
a dash!
It is getting quite
slow,
but whoa!
It turned the
corner, so insane.
You would think it
has lost its brain.
The flood plain now
is very calm,
so you shouldn't be alarmed.
And at last, finally,
it trickles slowly into the salty sea.

Phillip Jackson (10)
Denton West End Primary School

Easter

E ating chocolate Easter eggs
A ngels looking down on us on this happy day
S weetly toothaches for eating too much
T urning up to look at Jesus
E aster Day is just a happy day
R ainbow colours fall from the sky.

Kirsty Smith (9)
Denton West End Primary School

The River

Full and flowing
  everywhere,
    eroding banks
      here and there,
        children playing
          at the side,
            the river roars,
              they run and hide.

                Rivers race all through
              the night, waves are
                crashing left and right,
              wonderfully wet the
                water cripples, the
                  waterfall makes water
              ripple.

                Meanders creeping round the
              bend, tributaries never end.
            Streams trickle down the lane
          fields are drenched by the flood
plain.

Eleanor Jones (10)
Denton West End Primary School

Snow

I sit in the living room watching the snow,
The fire is on but still it is cold,
Little flakes fall from the sky,
I couldn't catch them all if I tried,
The sky is dark and so is the street,
The snow we are having is such a treat,
But then comes the sun and away goes the snow,
And it warms our bodies from head to toe.

Natasha Oliver (10)
Denton West End Primary School

Snow Poem

S oft as a kitten playing,
N oses freeze at wintertime,
O ver the cliffs it falls to the ground,
W hite as a cloud drifting away.
F alling from the sky,
L ying there waiting to be played with,
A dults shouting at children throwing snowballs at their houses,
K ing of the sky every year.
E veryone fighting and playing in the snow
S prinkling white icing all over the ground.

F rosty snowmen being built by children,
A s white as a horse galloping through frosty fields,
L ies a white cloak on the ground,
L aughing until the day ends.

    Forever will we not forget this day.
    Laughing and playing, that's all I can say.

Grace Alicia Higginbottom (9)
Denton West End Primary School

What Is It . . . ?

It's freezing like a freezer,
It shows your footprints,
It's white like white plain paper,
You can make things with it.
You can make angels.
You can make balls.
You can make walls.

So what is it?

Answer - Snow.

Joseph Carroll (9)
Denton West End Primary School

Snow

Snow falling on
the ground. Softly it
hits the ground. Cold on
people's feet. Shivering as
they wait. People rolling snow
making snowmen with their
hands. People feeling cold and
happy making walls of snow.
People throwing snowballs like
a hundred people. Everybody
cheering as it falls
down.

Snow is like a white
coat on the ground. Snowflakes
drifting in the sky as the clouds are
white. As you walk on the ground
the snow is cracking, making such a lovely
sound. As the snow melts on the
ground it looks like muddy slush.
As the snow goes, everybody's
sad, no more fun
anymore.

Christopher Hulme (9)
Denton West End Primary School

My Cool Car

My car is so cool,
It's great when I'm dropped off at school.
The leather seats are so mint,
I love the back window's silver tint.
The 20 inch alloys are so rad,
The chrome gear knob is so bad.
The sparkling spoiler is so bling,
My cool car is such an awesome thing.

Dominic Pimlott (11)
Denton West End Primary School

Animals

Animals, animals, cats and dogs, rabbits, hares, everywhere.
Animals, animals, you know they're all there.
There are all kinds of animals.
Animals are all around us.
They're fun to play with.
They're gentle and careful, sweet and kind,
We love animals.
Do you too?
We love animals, so do you.
We love animals, it's up to you.
Make your dreams come true.
Make your animal dreams come true too,
Animals are special and so are you!

Natalie Lovatt & Danielle Richardson (8)
Denton West End Primary School

The River

Water is rapid as it goes so fast
There is a splash and then a swift blast
River and streams flow into each other
So all of the salmon have to take cover
Water trickles down a tiny stream
The sun makes the crystal water gleam
Calm water swimming around
Then a steep drop straight to the ground
Splash, splosh
Falling into a water mound
It twists and turns around and round
One last bend and to the end
They're out to the . . . open sea!

Daniel Higham (11)
Denton West End Primary School

Fat Cat Milly

Milly was a black cat
She was very, very fat
All day long she sat
By the fire on her mat
Then one day her mother said,
'Milly, you are not getting fed,
You need to be able to chase the mice,
So from now on you will need to eat rice,
Then when you're thin
You will be able to chase the mice away from the bin.'

Luke Cooper & Patrick Lyons (8)
Denton West End Primary School

Dragons

A dragon is a disgusting one,
Except if they're friendly
They squirt out their boiling fire
I'm glad it's not a telephone wire
The raging fire blows out of its mouth.
Often they're all seen to be trouble
I'm glad I'm not one, if I was
I would be going *crunch, crunch, crunch,*
And eating you!

Melissa Wilson (8)
Denton West End Primary School

Love

L ovely boy, he jolly well is,
O h how he's handsome, so he is,
V odka we will drink all night,
E verybody sing and dance for the wedding prize!

Rebecca Taylor (8)
Denton West End Primary School

Pandora

Pandora the foal of magic
Who belongs to my sister and I
She was born in June, a day too soon
She was so small and shy.

Though June, July and August
She seemed to grow and grow
The work increased day by day
She kept us on the go.

Dad has to pay an awful lot
To keep her fit and trim
But if it keeps us happy
It's worth the world to him.

Laura Jones (10) & Rachel Jones (8)
Denton West End Primary School

Fireworks

Fireworks scream
Fireworks beam
Fireworks boom
Fireworks zoom
Fireworks screech
To the stars they can reach
The fireworks go fast
The fireworks go past
They light up the sky
So high they can fly
Fireworks go *bang!*
Fireworks go *clang!*

Sophie Rowen (8)
Denton West End Primary School

The River

Fast flowing forceful river. Wild wonderful wicked river,
Easing, tormenting, torturing ever becoming more calm and gentle
when all of a sudden

```
            D         D         D
            r         r         r
            o         o         o
            p         p         p
         splutter  splosh    spray
            splish    splash    splush
```

Trickling into the sea a calmly.   Tricking into a calmly.   Trickling into the sea a calmly.

Megan Dowse (10)
Denton West End Primary School

The River

Whistling
Water
diving
off the water
fall

It's freezing cold so I crouch up small
Watching the river as it carries on fast flowing
It's gone even colder now but I'm still going
Calming down
is the rapid rippling river
Looking at the icy water made me shiver
Meanders, swirling, round and round
Floods spreading on the ground
Flowing even slower to the mouth
Wave goodbye as the river flows south.

Alisha Street (11)
Denton West End Primary School

The River

Droplets of rain forming into a s   p   r
                                          t   o   u
                                          r   u   s
                                          e   r   h
                                          a   i   i
                                          m   n   n
                                                 g   g

Fast, fierce, flowing confluence approaching the tumble . . .
Calm ,slow, tender, glide with a gleam.

                    P
                    l
                    u
                    n
                    g
                    e

Quick, speedy, circular, swerve
Hit the bottom, splash, splosh.

Samantha Havern (10)
Denton West End Primary School

The River

Drip, drop goes the rain,
Rapid water swishing down and about.
Water hits, water splashing about.
Up high and in the air.
The water joins as one, gently.
Suddenly *plunge*.
Splashing, sploshing, splashing,
Racing to land.
Twisting, twirling, spinning around very slow,
Widening out, the sea is in reach.

Thomas Barr (10)
Denton West End Primary School

The River

Raining
rapidly
on the hills
    it   t   D   T
      r   r   a
   i   i   p
 c   p   p
k   p   i
l   i   n
e   n   g
s   g
    down and then it
    builds into the river
    as one, and then it
    just carries on and on.
     G
       e
         n
           t
           l
             y at first, getting
               to the waterfall
               but then it
                  d
                  r
                  o
                  p
                  s
               into a swirling, splashing round ball.
               Meandering it goes, but then slows.
               It slows right down and nearly stops
               and then you hear a great big *pop!*
               As the river hits the sea,
               now we can enjoy it, you and me.

Charlotte Dearden (11)
Denton West End Primary School

The River

The
water is
speedy
as it flows
so fast
huge amounts of water
come down in a blast
then the water comes to lash
and joins together
with a
ferocious
crash.

The river falls / of the / splashing / the plunge / with a pop pop

coming to a meander, going slow
looking at the water seeing it glow
at the delta the river turns into finger-like streams
into the sea and then it gleams.

Thomas Ellor (11)
Denton West End Primary School

The River

Splashing	Streams	Trickling
Splishing	Flowing	Speedily
In a rush	Rapidly	Down
To come	Together	The
Down		Mountain

Hastily spilling into a confluence
Pushing other streams about
Gaining speed and power
The river *roars* and *shouts*
Now the river comes together
Then

P P P P P P P
l l l l l l l
u u u u u u u
n n n n n n n
g g g g g g g
e e e e e e e

Splashing, struggling
Splishing, spraying
All about then out it goes
Getting slower by the minute
Into a flood plain

Trickle, trickle
Drifting out
Through the delta
Fingering its way to
The deep blue sea.

David Webb (10)
Denton West End Primary School

The River

Furiously spinning, swirling, rapidly
   as fast as a thunderbolt
      whirling, round and round

      g   s
      l   u
      e   n
      a   in the s
      m   h
      i   i
      n   n
      g   e

spinning, spectacular
shining and gleaming
    wildly
      s   s
      p   p
      l   l
      i   a
      s   s
      h   h

    raging
        glamorously
            shimmering
                glittery

      it's getting slower . . .

Rachael Postill (10)
Denton West End Primary School

Guppies

Whales have calves,
Dogs have puppies,
Horses have foals,
But guppies just have guppies!

Emma Raisbeck (9)
Denton West End Primary School

Food

Ham and cheese and mushy peas
Food, food, food
Sausage and chips and a haddock fish
Food, food, food
Carrots and beans and juicy seeds
Food, food, food
Apples and strawberries and big cherries
Food, food, food
Spaghetti and potatoes and large tomatoes
Food, food, food
We all need food!

Isabel O'Brien & Katie Savage (8)
Denton West End Primary School

Bonfire Night

B ang, bang, bang, boom, boom, boom,
A banging banger with a booming tune,
N ever-ending noise as it speeds through the sky,
G asping children with a squealing cry,
E ven playing with a dazzling light,
R ipping, soaring through the night.

Rachel Nield (10)
Denton West End Primary School

Seasons

S pring, summer, autumn, winter
E very month and every year
A utumn and winter - very cold
S pring and summer - very hot
O ver the year I am so happy, for seasons are great
N ow comes summer and spring
S oon autumn and winter.

Emily Haughton (9)
Denton West End Primary School

The Morning The World Was White . . .

When I looked through the window,
It looked like a white world,
Snow dancing peacefully down to the ground,
Untouched snow waiting to be trod on,
I put my wellies on and my thickest coat,
Then I put my soft gloves on and my woolly hat.

The snow was a white cloak,
And was bitingly cold,
As cold as ice,
Gleaming white snow,
What a magnificent sight,
I tasted the slushy, smooth snow,
It melted on my tongue.

In the park snowmen stood still, like an army,
Snowballs zooming through the air,
You could hear children laughing as they played,
Kids were sliding and gliding,
On the frozen pond,
What a wonderful experience!

Philip Kinder (10)
Denton West End Primary School

Concorde

14 wheels and its nose down
Leaving from Stockholm, Sweden
Picking up speed, brum, brum, brum
Over sea, supersonic
If you want to ride jump on it
Leather seat, look here's pilot Pete
Calling, 'Delta, Alpha'
Lands on its last flight.

Thanks Concorde!

Joseph Jones (9)
Denton West End Primary School

The River

The rain
f   g
 a   i   a
  l   t
   l   r   s
    s   a   o
      from grey clouds s   t   u
                                              r
                                                c
                                        e which
                                          w   f
                                          i   l
                                          l   o
                                          l   w
                               into the waterfall.
                   The waterfall
                   p
                   l   c
                   u   r
                   n   a
                   g   s   b
                   e   h   a
                   s   e   n
                        s   g
                              s
into the plunge pool
swiftly as it comes to the surface
it crashes through a confluence
f
o
l
l
o
w
s the meanders. The water trickles
down to the flood plains chasing children.
Finally off into the salty sea.

Daniel O'Connell (10)
Denton West End Primary School

Have You Ever Seen A Viking?

Once I saw a Viking
When I went out hiking
I tried to whack it with a twig
But he was very big
He wore his armour, very strong
I hardly dared to live for long
Its club was waving above my head
I really wished that I was in bed
Soon I found out that it was a dream
And then my eyes lit up with a gleam.

Emily Boggia (9)
Denton West End Primary School

Football

I love football
I think it's really great
When my mate shouts for the ball
I kick it with some weight.

The ref blows his whistle
And we all shout, 'Hooray
We've scored a goal
We have won the match today!'

Callum Dickson (8)
Denton West End Primary School

My Mum

My mum is the best
She deserves a rest
I will try my best
Not to be a pest
My mum's the best.

Matthew Smith (8)
Denton West End Primary School

The River

The cool
crashing river flows rapidly down until
(vertical: crashing / river / flows / rapidly / down / until)

           plunge
splash,   crash,
     splosh,   sprinkle
spray, tumble, weeping
      the river flows
       on and on
      while it meets
         the
       meanders
    twisting and turning
    winding, whirling
    round and round.
    Then it calms down
   continuing its journey
along the countryside to the
mouth which then meets the sea.

Kay Murfett (10)
Denton West End Primary School

Autumn Days

Autumn days when the grass is green.
The leaves turn different colours.
Conkers fall for children to collect.
Autumn days when rain comes hard.
Autumn days when it's hot and cold.
Autumn days when trees swing left and right.

James Scanlan (8)
Denton West End Primary School

The Morning The World Was White . . .

It's a winter wonderland,
Snow as soft as silk,
Down and down it comes.
Snow as white as milk,
Down and down it comes.
Elegant snow, graceful snow,
Down and down it comes.
Peaceful snow, gentle snow,
Down and down it comes.
Snow so glorious, snow so splendid,
Oh yes, it is a winter wonderland.

Jennifer Cowell (11)
Denton West End Primary School

Winter

Snow is crunching under your feet,
Children laughing as you build snowmen,
Snow is as white as a sheet,
People cheering as they throw away snowballs,
Adults listening in joy,
Snowflakes hitting you calmly on the cheek,
Snow drifting across the windy sky,
People sliding on the slippery ice,
Sledges sliding down mountains,
Sheets of snow sparkling like diamonds,
As soft as a piece of fur as you jump on it.

Sean Talbot (10)
Denton West End Primary School

The Morning The World Was White . . .

The snow is a white cloak,
The snow is falling, falling, falling,
And ice bracing as we play,
We are all having fun, fun, fun.

The snow is a white cloak,
As your cheeks go as red as a ruby,
And we are having fun,
And we are running, running, running.

And it is all elegant,
As we play, play, play.

Samantha Mitchell (10)
Denton West End Primary School

The Morning The World Was White . . .

Cold, cold snow falling all around,
A white cloak on the ground,
A magnificent, beautiful winter wonderland.

Its smooth, silky and velvety,
Crunching as it falls,
Snowflakes prancing and dancing,
Snow angels floating down.

Wool falling from the sky,
As cold as ice,
Its elegant beauty glistens for all to see.

Amy Pratt (10)
Denton West End Primary School

The River

The river running
rapidly from the
source, trying to
choose its new
course.

The tributary is like a stream joining to the
river, by finding a confluence.

The water is getting
wild, and the
weather isn't
mild.

The river is running
gently until there
is a sudden drop,
and when it hits
the plunge pool
you will hear a
splash.

The water trickles along as it gets to a flood plain
but if there is a heavy rainfall you will be in a flood.

The river is at the
mouth, and the waterfall
enters the sea, and now
the salt from the sea will
mix with the river water making it
tastes like the sea.

Karl Fairhurst (11)
Denton West End Primary School

The River

Rapid, fast
The flowing river trickling down the stream
Hitting the misty rocks. The river
Goes w
```
     i     i
     l     n
     d     t
           o  the c
                   o
                   n
                   f
                   l
                   u
                   e
                   n
                   c
                   e
```
Suddenly it speeds and slows
Up and down it firmly goes into
The waterfall racing
```
     i     t     m
     n     h     e
     t     e     a
     o           n
                 d
                 e
                 r
```
The river twists and turns
It finally slows and slows
Until it meets the sea.

Louis Ferguson (10)
Denton West End Primary School

The Morning The World Was White . . .

The frostbitten snowflakes swirled to the ground,
Leaving a blanket behind,
The elegant crisp and crackling snow.

Glistening gladly in the fresh air and light,
Getting faster each second,
Falling all around,
Trees outlined in an elegant white.

Snow shivering on the rooftops,
Fat snowmen whispering when they will be here next,
It feels so soft,
And tastes so flaky,
Untouched, but waiting for the battle to start.

Faye McInnes (11)
Denton West End Primary School

The River

Fast, full, flowing river
    winding, waving, wild water
        round rocks rapidly
    swishing, splashing, spraying, swirling
        down it comes,
    flowing here,
    flowing there,
    flowing nearly everywhere.
Slowing down, calming down,
    it starts to trickle into the deep blue sea.

Emma Schofield (11)
Denton West End Primary School

The River

Rapidly
flowing
wind blowing
erosion decaying
waves swaying.
The river's
  raging
    it can't stop!
      And now the river's
        about to
              d
              r
              o
              p
        The weeping waterfall's
          about to plunge
            into its pool. The water
              at the bottom so fresh,
                clean and cool.
                  The crazy meander
                swishes slowly around.
              The flood plain even
              slower, drenches the ground.
            It could flood the village,
           It could flood the town,
      but . . .no!
      The viscous river's slowing
      down. The water drifts
    as down to the delta
    as smooth as lotion,
   then trickles sluggishly
  into the ocean.

Victoria Hooton (10)
Denton West End Primary School

The River

Rivers,
  rivers
    all around
      bending
     round
    and
    round.
       As the
         water
           comes
             around
               children yell
            and stare!
        Thrashing
      and splashing
    all the time.
     People
      walking
       by and by.
        'Mummy,
          Mummy come
           here, I have
         found the
        end of
      the *river!*

         s!
       p
     l
    a
   s
  h
  i
 n
g

            Flowing splish, splash.

Katie Anne Lewis (11)
Denton West End Primary School

The River

Tiny droplets
    smooth, small
        silent. Stream
                f
               l
                 o
                   w
                     i
                    n
                      g
            along
                      s
                      p
                      l
                      a
                      s
            loud   h
                      i
                      n
                      g
        getting
        higher
              raucously
       softly
            as can be
f   t   r
l   h   i
o   e   v
o   e
d   r
i
n   b
g   a
          n
          k
then goes tearing past.

Charlotte Wilkins (10)
Denton West End Primary School

The River

The water
  comes gushing
    from down the
      mountain
        sometimes
          there will be
            fountain.

s   s
 p   p
  l   l
   i   o
    s   s
     h h

    Then the river starts
      to roar
        like fans do
          when football
            teams score.

            Rivers are
            racing all
            night through.
            Then the water
            soon becomes
            a drink for
            me or you!

crash   *bubble*
          meander
                              bobble.

Samuel Layne (11)
Denton West End Primary School

The River

So hasty and swift, nearly alarming
Speedy and smart, but not horrifying
    Shoving,
    Wild and awful, also erosion
    Soft
    But after that a lovely
        Emotion
        Slow and flowing at the
        t
        o
        p,
        very near to a deadly
            d
            r
            o
            p
        Swirling round a very big
                      b
                        e
                      n
                      d
    The pace so fast, will never lend.
    Calm, turning, very sluggish.
    Here is the mouth, a hand it could be,
    But all I know is that it leads to the sea.

Christopher McAllister (11)
Denton West End Primary School

The Morning The World Was White . . .

Laughter filling the packed air,
Snowballs flying here and there.
What a fabulous day,
We cheer, 'Hooray!'
Snowmen building,
Come out to play.

Snow parachuting through the air,
Play from dawn to the night,
Feast your eyes,
The snow is here,
Be careful on the roads,
It's not very clear,
Taste my snack covered in snow,
Feel the softness throw, throw, throw!

The snow is an enormous quivering quilt,
Lie on the ground and stay still.
A glistening glow makes me smile,
Build a humungous snow pile,
Make a fortress for me and you,
What's the password?
I don't have a clue.

Soon enough the snow will melt,
The sun will come out,
The fun will swell,
Better make the most of it.

Sam Burrows (10)
Denton West End Primary School

The Morning The World Was White . . .

Cold, cold snow falling on the ground,
Breath of ice,
And frosty spells,
Snow swirling in the trees,
Clouds of frost fill the air.

People making snowballs,
Glistening, gliding, sliding,
As I am walking round and round,
Snow is deeper than my feet,
I pick up the snow, it melts in my hands.

Crunch, crunch, crunch,
As I glide my way through the snow,
Decide to go sledging,
Smelling the crispy air,
Sliding down the hills, hills are white as fairies.

The snow was a blanket,
Perfect, puffy snow,
Crispy snow fills the air,
Slushy round my feet,
Wind whistling in my ear.

Rooftops full of crispy snow,
Smelling the crispy air,
Snowmen all around me,
Hope it snows tomorrow,
Hooray, hooray, it snowed today.

Erin Dickson (11)
Denton West End Primary School

The Morning The World Was White . . .

Snowflakes gently prance to the ground,
The winter wonderland is here.
The snow - a soft, crunchy, fresh blanket,
Glistening trees coated in a smooth, flaky masterpiece.
Soft, silent, still,
Falling all around.
Crisp snowflakes swirl to the shore below.
Frozen icy ponds everywhere.
Crunching softly under my feet,
Snow angels ascended from Heaven.

Bethany Mullarkey (10)
Denton West End Primary School

The Morning The World Was White . . .

Glistening coats of white,
Lying on the ground,
As wet wellies squelch into the snow,
Elegant, soft surroundings cover the earth,
Six snowmen standing proud,
Underneath a rain cloud,
Peaceful noises all around,
As snow dances on the ground,
Frosty feet, cold toes,
As cold as ice.

Thomas Thorpe (11)
Denton West End Primary School

The Morning The World Was White . . .

The snow glistening like a cloud,
Swirling in the trees,
Shimmering on the rooftops,
Me and my friends skidding on the icy ponds,
The snow mounting higher and higher,
Like a silver carpet.

The freezing snow pearly-white,
The snow was a blanket,
Glistening like a diamond,
The slush biting into my cold hands,
Making snow angels continuously,
My face as red as a ruby.

Snowballs catching my coat as I walk,
Snowmen rolling like a ball,
Sledging, sliding and gliding,
Frosty spells,
And a breath of ice,
Blowing into my hair.

Wind whispering my woolly scarf,
Snowballs thrown at the back of my head,
Ice clinging to the walls like icicles,
Sliding on the silver carpet,
The snow swirling,
Softly, swiftly, silently.

Charlotte Williams (10)
Denton West End Primary School

Monkey Poem

Some monkeys are big and strong,
But some monkeys are small and long.
High in the trees the monkeys swing,
From branch to branch, what a wonderful thing.
All monkeys walk,
But they don't talk.
Monkeys always play,
But they never eat hay.
The monkeys eat fleas,
But they don't eat bees.

Rebecca Oliver (7)
Denton West End Primary School

Night Wind

The wind whistles in the wintry night
As trees swish side to side
The grass sways on the pavement
As leaves fly off trees
The people crash and crash the brown leaves.

The smooth wind slides across your face
The butterflies land on dark, green leaves
Worms slide through the mud
The people play in the rain still purring and purring.

While the people snuggle in their beds
The animals snuggle up where they are
But soon they will be away in another place
The star flashes through the night
The bushes move and move.

Snakes slide through the dry, warm grass
They eat their prey as they hunt them down
Soon it will be night again.

Daryll Alladice (9)
Haveley Hey Primary School

Anything's Possible

If dogs could talk,
And dinosaurs were alive,
If whales could walk,
And if ships could fly.

If babies rode motorbikes,
And if the moon came out in the day,
If Earth was called Pluto,
And robbers refused to rob.

If cars weren't invented,
And cats were in-charge,
If humans were animals,
And letters were numbers.

If you read this poem,
That doesn't make any sense,
If you laugh and giggle,
There is no offence.

Nathan Frazer & Steven Hayhurst
Haveley Hey Primary School

The Traveller

The traveller came from a village in the forest.
He wore a brown cloak and his lips were red as tomatoes.
His horse was grey and loved to chomp the grass.
The traveller had no answer to his knock at the house, so dark.
There was no breath or movement inside the house.
The stars twinkled in the sky above.
The traveller knocked but there was no answer again.
The birds on the roof flew away as the traveller and his horse returned sadly to their village.

Chloe Pritchard (8)
Haveley Hey Primary School

Happy Mother's Day

H appy Mother's Day
A bsolutely kind
P retty face
P retty mother
Y ou're the best

M um, you're great
O h you are nice
T o Mum, you're fab
H ow are you today?
E very day I love you more
R oses are red, violets are blue, you are as cuddly
   as Winnie the Pooh
S plendid house

D airy Milk chocolate just for you
A re you the best?
Y es you are.

Harlie Burgess (10)
Haveley Hey Primary School

The Listeners

Along came a traveller one day
Knocking on a moonlit door
All dressed in black and white
Like a newspaper
He carried a big suitcase
He wanted a place to take a nap
No one would let him sleep
Inside the house the people
Were listening to his cry in silence.

Patience Owens (9)
Haveley Hey Primary School

The Listeners

He covered his sack with oak leaves
And filled it with conkers for defence.

He was as tall as a tree
And as thin as a stick.

His pale face was
As if he had seen a ghost.

He fiddled with his wedding ring
Because he missed his wife a lot.

He had teeth, rotten as sour milk,
His hair was as black as a panther.

His cloak was as black
As the darkness around him.

Paige Dyson (9)
Haveley Hey Primary School

A Catalogue To Make Me A . . .

A boulder-taker
A oxbow-maker

An alligator-cooler
A rain-fooler

A meander-maker
A land-shaper

A mountain-slider
A sea-finer.

A catalogue to make me a river.

Jake Grady (11)
Haveley Hey Primary School

The Listeners

From the middle of the stairs came a creak.
Cats screeched from behind the moonlit house.
The traveller's heart beat like the horse's hooves,
The stranger quickly melted into the silence.
The curtains twitched quickly,
But then quickly froze in the moonlight.
The stranger's horse chomped on the grass
Like a child munching a chocolate bar.

Adam Locklin (9)
Haveley Hey Primary School

Sweets

Swirly snakes
Swizzly cakes
After Eights
Strawberry lace
Black bonbons
Sweet Haribo
All my favourite sweets!

Adam Mayes (10)
Haveley Hey Primary School

The Blue Waterfall

Down and down the water falls
Jumping and dancing as it falls,
Twisting and turning down an down as it hits the bottom
Crashing and bashing sounds as it hits the ground
Down and down the water falls
Crashing, bashing, twisting and turning as it falls.

Lisa Bond (10)
Haveley Hey Primary School

The Sparkling Waterfall

It rushes towards me like a leopard
Trying to pounce on his prey.

My ears pop at the sound of the waterfall
Streaming down like the sound of thunder.

The waterfall twinkles like a star
Lighting up the sky.

Then like a twister gathers speed
And makes me feel dizzy.

Chloe Smith (10)
Haveley Hey Primary School

My Waterfall Poem

As I look up at this huge beast I feel tiny.
The sunlight sparkles on the waterfall.
It is as beautiful as a butterfly.
I feel peaceful and calm.
It sounds like thunder and torpedoes launched.

Ainsley Gittings (10)
Haveley Hey Primary School

Colours

Silver is the colour of my dad's BMW.
Blue is the colour of City's kit.
Brown is the colour of Nicolas Anelka.
Red is the colour of David James' socks.
Black is the colour of my PS2.
White is the colour of Jay Jay Okocha's shirt.
Orange is the colour of Wolves' shirts.
Yellow is the colour of Ronaldinio's Brazil shirt.

Joshua Butterworth (9)
Manchester Road Primary School

At The Bottom Of The Ocean

At the bottom of the ocean I can see . . .

Ten tiny turtles swimming like divers
Nine naughty Nemos playing like children
Eight enormous eels electrocuting like sockets
Seven slimy water snakes rolling like roller coasters
Six scary sharks snapping like castanets
Five funny frogs flexing like acrobats
Four friendly fish flapping fins like a seal
Three transparent tadpoles sleeping like babies
Two terrifying terrapins floating like paper
One shimmering treasure chest opened like a fridge door.

Sophie Stockton (9)
Manchester Road Primary School

At The Bottom Of The Ocean

At the bottom of the ocean I can see . . .
Ten tall turtles like the five of you
Nine naughty Nemos swimming like Ian Thorpe
Eight cranky crawfish like old whales
Seven snappy turtles snapping like sharks
Six slithering eels like jelly
Five crunchy crabs like a Crunchie bar
Four slimy bits of seaweed swaying about
Three scary sharks that look like monsters
Two freckly frogs jumping like mad
One humungous box of treasure lying around.

Mully Kempson (8)
Manchester Road Primary School

At The Bottom Of The Ocean

At the bottom of the ocean I can see . . .
Ten shimmering starfish swaying like swans
Nine tiny turtles swimming like frogs
Eight slimy sea snakes spinning like children
Seven smooth shells getting pushed like prams
Six disguised divers swimming like fish
Five jolly jellyfish jumping like kangaroos
Four elegant eels twirling like washing machines
Three naughty Nemos getting lost like sheep
Two sly sharks hunting like huntsmen
One glittery treasure chest waiting to be opened.

Jay Ogden (8)
Manchester Road Primary School

At The Bottom Of The Ocean

At the bottom of the ocean I can see . . .
Ten creepy crabs pinching like crayfish
Nine naughty Nemos swimming like Ian Thorpe
Eight electric eels eating like elephants
Seven slimy stingrays swaying like swans
Six snappy tortoises snapping like sharks
Five flexible frogs flexing like acrobats
Four funny fish swimming like ducks
Three tiny turtles biting like clownfish
Two tiny tadpoles teaching like teachers
One gigantic blue whale swimming slowly like a giant turtle.

Ryan Watson (9)
Manchester Road Primary School

At The Bottom Of The Ocean

At the bottom of the ocean I can see . . .

Ten tiny turtles swimming like divers,
Nine naughty Nemos playing like clowns,
Eight enormous eels electrocuting like sockets
Seven slimy water snakes rolling like a roller coast
Six scary sharks snapping like castanets
Five funny frogs flexing like gymnasts
Four friendly fish flapping fins like a seal
Three transparent tadpoles sleeping like babies
Two terrifying terrapins snapping like sharks
One glistening treasure chest glittering like diamonds.

Danielle Scott (8)
Manchester Road Primary School

At The Bottom Of The Ocean

At the bottom of the ocean I can see . . .

Ten terrifying turtles resting like babies
Nine naughty Nemos getting shouted at like children
Eight golden earrings sunken like ships
Seven silly starfish swaying like waves
Six smiling swordfish fighting like pirates
Five foolish frogs joking like jesters
Four fat foxes hunting like dogs (near the sea)
Three thin fish swimming like swimmers
Two tangled wrecked ships staying there like a piece of concrete
One sparkling treasure chest, golden like a diamond.

Charlotte Murray (8)
Manchester Road Primary School

At The Bottom Of The Ocean

At the bottom of the ocean I can see . . .

Ten silly clownfish swimming like a swimmer
Nine shimmering starfish fast asleep
Eight basking sharks pulling their faces
Seven electric eels electrocuting the fish
Six dancing dolphins playing like children
Five funny frogs flexing like an acrobat
Four hunting hammerheads hunting like a farmer
Three sharp swordfish fighting like a knight
Two silly sea horses bouncing like a ball
One big treasure chest shining like the stars.

Connie Blakey (8)
Manchester Road Primary School

At The Bottom Of The Ocean

At the bottom of the ocean I can see . . .

Ten tiny turtles flapping like birds
Nine naughty Nemos swimming like a motorboat
Eight electric eels electrocuting like sockets
Seven sets of seaweed swaying like the breeze
Six slimy sea snakes slithering like boa constrictors
Five fat frogs jumping like kangaroos
Four hunting hammerheads spying like foxes
Three threatening sharks teasing like bullies
Two sly swordfish fighting like knights
One gleaming treasure chest sparkling like gold.

Callum McCartney (8)
Manchester Road Primary School

My Life

What will be
Left here for me
When I grow up?

Will there be
Oxygen?
Will the air be clean?

Will there be
Animals roaming around?
Will the trees be green?

Will there be
Fresh food to eat?
Will it be clean to eat?

Will there be
Trees to give us shade?
Will there be flowers beneath our feet?

Laurence Giles (8)
Manchester Road Primary School

Five Little Animals

Five little dogs sitting on the wall
One fell off and then there were four.

Four little cats sitting in a tree
One bought a takeaway and then there were three.

Three little birds sitting on the loo
One fell in and then there were two.

Two little crabs sitting on a swan
One had gone and then there was one.

One little swan playing with a bomb
It blew up and then there was none.

Christopher Walker (9)
Manchester Road Primary School

My Future

What will be
Left here for me
When I grow up?

Will there be
Water to drink?
Will houses still stand?

Will there be
Jobs for me
And beautiful flowers?

Will there be
Trees still standing
To give oxygen.

Will there be cars
When I grow up?
Will there be schools?

Callum Olliver (8)
Manchester Road Primary School

At The Bottom Of The Ocean

At the bottom of the ocean I can see . . .

Ten amazing anglerfish swimming softly
Nine jolly jellyfish jumping like jelly beans
Eight electric eels electrocuting like sockets
Seven silly swordfish savaging like robbers
Six salty salamanders bathing like lazy people
Five dolly dolphins playing like children
Four soft sea turtles snapping like crocodiles
Three sharks swaying like swans
Two stingrays burying like crabs
One ginormous treasure chest sparkling like diamonds.

Alix Allbrighton (8)
Manchester Road Primary School

My Future

What will be
left for me
when I grow up?

Will there be
cats and dogs
and toys to play with?

Will there be
hospitals and nutritious
cereal to eat?

Will there be
cars and buses
and bikes and trains?

Will there be
technology and computers
and fun games?

Jack Barnes (9)
Manchester Road Primary School

Five Little Men

Five little men running at the door,
one tripped over then there were four.

Four little men working on a tree,
one fell off then there were three.

Three little men sitting on a loo,
one fell in then there were two.

Two little men playing with a bomb,
one got blown up then there was one.

One little man playing on a swan,
he fell in, then there were none.

Lloyd Simpson (10)
Manchester Road Primary School

My Future

What will be
Left here for me
When I grow up?

Will there be
Food to eat
And animals to feed?

Will there be
Water to drink
And toys to play with?

Will there be
People to talk to
And shops to buy from?

Will there be
Cars and buses
Trams and trains?

Will there be
Friends to play with
And places to go.

Courtney Clarke (8)
Manchester Road Primary School

Colours

Red is the colour of a brand new car
Red is the colour of some tar
Yellow is the colour of someone's face
Yellow is the colour of someone's lace
Orange is the colour of my teacher's book
Orange is the colour of my friend's hook
Black is the colour of a nice suit
Black is the colour of a flute
Gold is the colour of a fish
Gold is the colour of a famous dish.

David Broome (10)
Manchester Road Primary School

My Future

What will be
left here for me
when I grow up?

Will there be
fish still swimming
happily in the river?

Will there be
trees, insects and plants
still alive?

Will there be
enough houses
for people to live in?

Will there still be
enough food and drinks
for animals and people?

Victoria Haining (8)
Manchester Road Primary School

My Pet Puppy

She is cute
She is furry
She is kind
She is mine.

She is silky
She is playful
She is lovely
She's my pet puppy.

She is cuddly
She is golden
She is a gentle puppy
    And that's my puppy.

Amy Crowley (10)
Manchester Road Primary School

My Future

What will be
left here for me
when I grow up?

Will there be
books to read
and authors to write them?

Will there be
schools to learn in
and friends to be there for you?

Will there be
shops to buy from
and money to pay?

Will there be
clothes to wear
and shoes to put on your feet?

Will there be
water to drink
and food to keep us alive?

Francesca Hodson-Ridgway (9)
Manchester Road Primary School

Colours

Blue is the colour of City's home ground
Green is the colour of the swaying grass
Red is the colour of a red rose
Yellow is the colour of the sun shining bright
Orange is the colour of fizzy Fanta
Purple is the colour of a violet
Gold is the colour of a one pound coin
Black is the colour of James Bond's suit
White is the colour of our school T-shirt
Brown is the colour of a brown piece of wood.

Bethan Redman (10)
Manchester Road Primary School

Ten Happy Men

Ten happy men
Working in a mine
One caught fire
And then there were nine

Nine happy men
Playing football
One got kicked
And then there were eight

Eight happy men
Going to Heaven
On their way one lost their wing
And then there were seven

Seven happy men
Doing tricks
One got chopped in half
And then there were six

Six happy men
Looking for wives
One got jumped
And then there were five

Five happy men
On a tour
One got shot
And then there were four

Four happy men
Playing a game
One needed the toilet
And then there were three

Three happy men
Playing Guess Who
One lost
And then there were two

Two happy men
Playing a game
One was called Ron
And then there was one

One happy man
All alone
And then there were none.

Kyle Howles (10)
Manchester Road Primary School

The Nintendo Gamecube

Racing with Mario,
Busting games with Bowser,
Sucking up ghosts with Luigi,
And fighting monsters with Waluigi.

The Nintendo Gamecube is the best
It's way better than the rest.
You can now buy it for less,
So the Gamecube is the best!

Joe Blakey (11)
Manchester Road Primary School

10 Little Frogs

Ten little frogs
Jumping on a log
One broke his spine
And then there were nine

Nine little frogs
Used as bait
One got caught
And then there were eight

Eight little frogs
Going to Heaven
One got lost
And then there were seven

Seven little frogs
Jumping on sticks
One got tramped on
And then there were six

Six little frogs
Swimming in a pond
One learnt to dive
And then there were five

Five little frogs
Jumping through a door
One got smacked
And then there were four

Four little frogs
Cutting tree
One got crushed
And then there were three

Three little frogs
All being heroes
They all broke their legs
Then there was zero.

Jordan Thompson (9)
Manchester Road Primary School

Colours And Animals

Colours
Blue is the colour of salty sea,
Red is the colour of an angry me.
Green is the colour of Libya's flag,
Black is the colour of a Gucci bag.
Pink is the colour of a squealing pig,
Purple is the colour of a silly wig.
Gold is the colour of a fancy ring,
White is he colour of a sick king.
Silver is the colour of misty moon,
I've got to go, I'll see you soon.

Animals
Dogs sit around eating bones,
While birds have such lovely tones.
Cats run around chasing mice,
And rabbits are just so, so nice.
Fish do absolutely nothing at all,
Giraffes are just so, so tall.
Elephants have such long trunks,
The smelly ones are obviously skunks.
Horses are beautiful head to toe,
Zebras are a lion's foe.
Kangaroos are attached to their mother,
But they're all as beautiful as each other.

Elizabeth Fenwick (10)
Manchester Road Primary School

Colours

Blue is the colour of my best team
Yellow is the colour of vanilla ice cream
Green is the colour I see in my dreams
White is the colour of a lot of steam
Black is the colour of a spider so mean
Red is the colour of a laser beam
Purple is the colour of the place I've been.

Thomas Lawlor (10)
Manchester Road Primary School

Animal Poem

Imagine a snake,
Thin as a steak.

Imagine a pig,
Wearing a wig.

Imagine a dog
In the fog.

Imagine a flea,
Eating me.

Imagine a bear,
In underwear.

Imagine a cat,
Eating a hat.

Imagine a giraffe,
Having a laugh.

Imagine a seal,
Eating a meal.

Rachel Hammersley (8)
Manchester Road Primary School

All Sorts

A cute cat, a big, fat rat
A blue sky, birds that fly
An angry teacher, a hungry creature
A long, dirty log, a big, cute dog
A broken box, a hairy fox
A huge bear, a green pear
A small bag, a big flag
A small jug, a fat slug.

Ashleigh Duty (9)
Manchester Road Primary School

Colours

Red is the colour of a library chair
Bronze is the colour of my friend's hair.
Blue is the colour of our uniform
Green is the colour of my brother's horn.
Silver is the colour of a ten pence,
Brown is the colour of my fence.
Grey is the colour of the water's edge,
White is the colour of my mum's window ledge.
Orange is the colour of a big ripe bun,
Black is the colour of James Bond's gun.
Gold is the colour of my trophies,
Pink is the colour of some toffees.
Yellow is the colour of a piece of card,
I think my homework is really hard.
Peach is the colour of a bright new face,
See you soon, I'm winning the race.

Ashlie Ball (10)
Manchester Road Primary School

My Pet

She is silky
She is kind
She is furry
She is mine

She is cute
She is soft
She is only
My pet dog

She is golden
She is fun
She is the colour
Of the setting sun.

Christie Marsh (9)
Manchester Road Primary School

Colours

Yellow is the colour of Winnie the Pooh
Blue is the colour of a jumping dolphin
Pink is the colour of my socks
Red is the colour of my dress.

Green is the colour of the grass growing high
Black is the colour of my school shoes
Orange is the colour of a carrot
Purple is the colour of violets.

Jodie Wilson (10)
Manchester Road Primary School

Colours

I don't know anything that's purple
But I do know something that's blue
I think I know something that's pink
It's the colour of me and you
Green is the colour of my toy town
Can you think of anything that's brown?
Red is the colour of our lips
Giving your Mum and dad a kiss.

Amy Schofield (9)
Manchester Road Primary School

Nature

Nature is a marvellous thing,
everywhere you go you can hear birds sing.
Life and peace is always there,
some people in the world don't even care.
Flowers and trees they will still grow,
you know that and I know so.
Animals live in forest and seas,
what makes honey? Of course it's bees!

Rachel Gill (9)
Manchester Road Primary School

Ten Happy Teddies

Ten happy teddies
Were all feeling fine
One teddy went somewhere else
Then there were nine

Nine happy teddies
Going on a date
One teddy didn't show
Then there were eight

Eight happy teddies
Travelling to Devon
One teddy didn't feel well
Then there were seven

Seven happy teddies
Playing with some bricks
One fell on a teddy's toe
Then there were six

Six happy teddies
Going for a dive
One couldn't swim
Then there were five

Five happy teddies
Fixing a door
One teddy hurt his thumb
Then there were four

Four happy teddies
Making some tea
One teddy scalded itself
Then there were three

Three happy teddies
Messing with the glue
One teddy got fed up
Then there were two

Two happy teddies
Playing in the sun
One teddy got too hot
Then there was one

One happy teddy
All on his own
It's not sad really
Because he just walked back home.

Lauren Scott (10)
Manchester Road Primary School

Animal Poem

Imagine a snake
thin as a rake.

Imagine a pig
wearing a wig.

Imagine a dog
playing with a frog.

Imagine a flea
chasing me.

Imagine a bear
being a mayor.

Imagine a cat
having a chat.

Imagine a giraffe
having as bath.

Imagine a seal
eating a meal.

Danielle Kenny (9)
Manchester Road Primary School

Animal Poem

Imagine a snake
Thin as a rake

Imagine a pig
With a wig

Imagine a dog
Eating in the fog

Image a flee
Chasing me

Imagine a bear
At the fair

Imagine a cat
With a bat

Imagine a giraffe
In the bath

Imagine a seal
With a wheel.

Dane Oliver (9)
Manchester Road Primary School

Lightning

Lightning flashes in the night
Making an enormous noise
It strikes down trees
And dark clouds gather when it begins to rain.

The sky is dark
The lightning flashes
As it rumbles in the night
Rain pouring down
Hitting at the floor
As lightning crashes in the night.

Sarah Newsham (11)
Manchester Road Primary School

Five Little Turtles

Five little turtles crawling on the beach
One of them walked to the shore
And then there were four

Four little turtles crawling on the beach
One of them walked to the sea
And then there were three

Three little turtles crawling on the beach
One of them got stuck in a shoe
And then there were two

Two little turtles crawling on the beach
One of them threw a bomb
And then there was one

One little turtle crawling on the beach
It has gone -
And then there were none.

Andrei Howles (9)
Manchester Road Primary School

Five Big Cobra Snakes

Five big cobra snakes slithering in the desert
One of them went to the store
And then there were four.
Four big cobra snakes slithering in the desert
One of them got stung by a bee
And then there were three.
Three big cobra snakes slithering in the desert
One said, 'Boo!'
And then there were two.
Two big cobra snakes slithering in the desert
One threw a bomb
And then there was one.
One big cobra snake slithering in the desert
It jumped on a swan
And then there were none!

Shaun Booth (9)
Manchester Road Primary School

Ten Little Street Racers

Ten little street racers zooming down the line
One popped his tyre
And then there were nine!

Nine little street racers all meeting at the gate
One was late
And then there were eight!

Eight little street racers racing around Devon
One blew his engine
And then there were seven!

Seven little street racers going over bricks
One went too high
And then there were six!

Six little street racers having a drive
One drove into a beehive
And then there were five!

Five little street racers sliding on the floor
One exploded
And then there were four!

Four little street racers needed a wee
One couldn't face it
And then there were three!

Daniel Rowland (11)
Manchester Road Primary School

Colours

Green is the colour of my dad's car
Gold is the colour of a star.
Yellow is the colour of an Egyptian tomb,
Blue is the colour of my bedroom.
Silver is the colour of lead,
White is the colour of bread.
Black is the colour of my dad's tyre,
Orange is the colour of the fire.

Liam Shannon (9)
Manchester Road Primary School

Animal Poem

Imagine a snake,
Thin as a cake.

Imagine a pig,
Wearing a wig.

Imagine a dog,
Chewing a log.

Imagine a flea,
Having tea.

Imagine a bear,
At the fair.

Imagine a cat,
In a flat.

Imagine a giraffe,
Having a laugh.

Imagine a seal,
Eating a meal.

Kieran Lee (7)
Manchester Road Primary School

My Future

What will be left here for me
when I grow up?

Will there be water to drink?
Electricity to use?

Will there be shops and money -
and food to eat?

Will there be milk from cows -
milk for goodness?

Daniel Pridding (8)
Manchester Road Primary School

Ten Bossy Teachers

Ten bossy teachers, drinking wine
One got drunk
And then there were nine

Nine bossy teachers got in late
One got scared
And then there were eight

Eight bossy teachers went to Devon
One got lost
And then there were seven

Seven bossy teachers eating pic 'n' mix
One got toothache
And then there were six

Six bossy teachers learning how to dive
One drowned
And then there were five

Five bossy teachers walking into a door
One went the wrong way
And then there were four

Four bossy teachers sitting by the sea
One got eaten by a shark
And then there were three

Three bossy teachers went to the loo
One could not hold it
And then there were two

Two bossy teachers sitting in the sun
One got sunburned
And then there was one

One bossy teacher all alone
She went for a cup of tea
And then there were none!

Anne-Marie Holmes (10)
Manchester Road Primary School

Ten Little Puppies

Ten little puppies went into the mine
One got lost
And then there were nine

Nine little puppies put on weight
One got too fat
And then there were eight

Eight little puppies went up to Heaven
One fell over
And then there were seven

Seven little puppies playing with sticks
One got hurt
And then there were six

Six little puppies saw a beehive
One got stung
And then there were five

Five little puppies walked through the door
One shut the door
And then there were four

Four little puppies climbed up the tree
One got stuck
And then there were three

Three little puppies washing in the loo
One got poisoned
And then there were two

Two little puppies staring at Ron
One ran off
And then there was one

One little puppy, had a broken bone
He never recovered
And then there were none!

Chloe Smith (10) & Louise Edwards (11)
Manchester Road Primary School

Ten Little Choirboys

Ten little choirboys singing a rhyme
One lost his voice
And then there were nine

Nine little choirboys losing weight
One got too skinny
And then there were eight

Eight little choirboys all twenty-seven
One got too old
And then there were seven

Seven little choirboys eating Weetabix
One got addicted
And then there were six

Six little choirboys feeling alive
One dropped down dead
And then there were five

Five little choirboys singing more
One felt tired
And then there were four

Four little choirboys singing merrily
One couldn't breath
And then there were three

Three little choirboys putting on their shoes
One couldn't tie the lace
And then there were two

Two little choirboys playing with a time-bomb
One got knocked over
And then there was one

One little choirboy chasing Tom
He got bored
And then there were none.

Damon Hale & Craig Bradley (10)
Manchester Road Primary School

Ten Little Puppies

Ten little puppies running in a line
One fell over
Then there were nine

Nine little puppies all losing weight
One got too thin
Then there were eight

Eight little puppies all went to Devon
One got a girlfriend
Then there were seven

Seven little puppies all doing tricks
One broke his leg
Then there were six

Six little puppies all were alive
One got pneumonia
Then there were five

Five little puppies all chewing the door
One got a splinter
Then there were four

Four little puppies all needed a wee
One wet himself
Then there were three

Three little puppies all had the flu
One died
Then there were two

Two little puppies playing with Tom
One got too rough
Then there was one

One little puppy all on its own
He got picked on
Then there were none.

Leah Jordan (10)
Manchester Road Primary School

The Sky

That sun up there
In the summer sky
All hot
On a frosty day
That golden sun
Sheds a blinding light.

That moon up there
In the August dusk
When moths are drawn
To the window's light
That pale old moon
Is a marvellous sight.

That star up there
It caught my eye
Sparkling so bright
You couldn't miss it
It shimmers in the moonlight.

Samuel Richardson (10)
Manchester Road Primary School

Colours

Green is the colour of the grass,
Red is the colour of fire.
Silver is the colour of my penny,
Gold is the colour of the sun.
Brown is the colour of beers in the pub,
Blue is the colour of the sky.
Yellow is the colour of my colouring pencil
Black is the colour of the leopard's spots.
Pink is the colour of a rose,
That's why I like colours.

Reece Tittensor & Nathan Oldham (10)
Manchester Road Primary School

Ten Little Footballs

Ten little footballs standing in a line
One fell off, then there were nine

Nine little footballs on a plate
One got popped, then there were eight

Eight little footballs going to Devon
One fell off the boat, then there were seven

Seven little footballs picking up sticks
One fell over, then there were six

Six little footballs playing with a beehive
One got stung, then there were five

Five little footballs knocked at the door
One knocked too hard, then there were four

Four little footballs climbed a tree
One got stuck, then there were three

Three little footballs all had the flu
One died, then there were two

Two little footballs had a bomb
It exploded, then there was one

One little football all the rest had gone
He went in, then there were none.

Jessica Husband (10)
Manchester Road Primary School

Dogs

Dogs, dogs all around
In the park and in the playground
Dogs are so sweet
They love to eat meat
They run dead fast after the ball
Some are really big and some are dead small
Some jump really high
Some dogs, just like to lie.

Jade Leah Scrivner (9)
Manchester Road Primary School

Ten Happy Lions

Ten happy lions
Standing in a line
One fell over
Then there were nine.

Nine happy lions
Making new mates
One fell out, straight away
Then there were eight

Eight happy lions
Eating a melon
One ate too much
Then there were seven

Seven happy lions
Collecting sticks
One poked himself in the eye
Then there were six

Six happy lions
Staring at a hive
One got bored
Then there were five

Five happy lions
On the seashore
One started collecting shells
Then there were four

Four happy lions
Teasing a bee
One saw it get angry
Then there were three

Three happy lions
Chewing on a shoe
One sniffed its smell
Then there were two

Two happy lions
Watching Pokémon
One got scared
Then there was one

One happy lion
Playing as the sun shone
He got hungry
Then there were none!

Abigail Surridge (9)
Manchester Road Primary School

Animals

Monkey

The monkey, so agile and quick,
gives his little tail a flick.
He swings round from branch to branch
doing his own little dance.
Thinks about food all day and night,
nothing to give him a fright.

Elephant

The elephant, so big and slow,
thinks about how much food to go.
His trunk, so long and slender so,
grows all day and night.
His feet so huge and hard to move,
come down like a bellyflop in a swimming pool.

Cheetah

The cheetah, fastest animal on Earth
runs so fast, he's hard to catch.
He's spotted by a hunter
ready to kill.
Poor cheetah, going to die
from another hunter's skill.

Jack Steed (10)
Manchester Road Primary School

My Favourite Animals

Dogs like to run round and round
Dogs lay quietly on the ground
Dogs are big and dogs are small
Dogs like to climb on the garden wall
I love dogs!

Fish can swim around and around
Fish do not make a sound
Fish enjoy eating their food
Fish like to play, if they're in the mood
I love fish!

Budgies like to squawk
Budgies try to talk
Budgies like to fly in the room
Budgies do not bark or boom
I love budgies!

Alannah Stockton (11)
Manchester Road Primary School

Five Little Gymnasts

Five little gymnasts coming through the door,
One got squashed and then there were four.

Four little gymnasts eating tea, one choked
And then there were three.

Three little gymnasts trying to find a shoe,
One got lost and then there were two.

Two little gymnasts riding on a swan,
One fell off and then there was one.

One little gymnast messing with a bomb,
She exploded and then there were *none!*

Jessica Murphy (9)
Manchester Road Primary School

Manchester United

United are the best
Better than all the rest
The day has come
United versus the worst team in the world
City!
Ten minutes into the game
City gets a penalty,
Howard saves Anelka's shot,
Scholes passes to
Ruud Van Nistelrooy
He shoots from forty yards out.
Calamity James misses
Goal!
1 - 0 to United
Van Nistelrooy passes to Saha
Who shoots . . .
Goal!
(Calamity James misses again)
Anelka fouls Ronaldo
Anelka gets a red car
The match has ended 2 - 0
To the *Devils!*

Adam Atherton (11)
Manchester Road Primary School

The Big Game

Today is the day of the big game,
United and City yet again!
Alex wants to win the cup,
Kevin's got the hiccups,
Ronaldo runs for a goal,
Scores! Oh a beautiful goal.
The final score is 4-2,
Just the best for me and you.

Katie Pridding (11)
Manchester Road Primary School

Animal Poem

Imagine a snake,
Thin as a cake.

Imagine a pig,
Wearing a wig.

Imagine a dog,
Nudging a log.

Imagine a flea,
Having a wee.

Imagine a bear,
In underwear.

Imagine a cat,
Having a flat.

Imagine a giraffe,
Taking a bath.

Imagine a seal,
Eating a wheel.

Kyle Lowe (7)
Manchester Road Primary School

Football

F ootball, football is the best,
O ur defender is a pest,
O w, what a nasty fall,
T homas Taylor is on the ball.
B radleigh does a good header,
A dam thinks he can do better.
L iam shoots and hits the pole,
L arry makes a wonderful goal.

Craig Taylor (10)
Manchester Road Primary School

Teachers

Old Mr Park,
Walks about in the dark.

New Mrs Can,
Always cooks in a pan.

Good Mr Cook,
Is never seen without a book.

Nice Mrs Dice,
Hates nasty mice.

Horrible Mr Spot,
Sleeps in a cot.

Stupid Miss Mat,
Hit herself with a bat.

Sensible Mr Tray,
Goes to church to pray.

Silly Miss Mable,
Dances on the table.

Flexible Mr Bend,
Says 'It's the end.'

Jessica Hyde (11)
Manchester Road Primary School

Night

At night I hear the sound of feet,
As I walk down the scary street.
Then I hear a dog bark,
As I turn into the park.
I look up at the stars above,
And see a cloud shaped like a dove,
Then I hear somebody shout,
And I run for a way out!
Now I'm at home in my bed,
Ready to rest my sleepy head.

Holly Prescott (11)
Manchester Road Primary School

City's Victory

Today is the day,
City and United play,
Last time,
City scored nine.

Anelka shoots,
Of course he'll score,
All the fans shout,
'We want more!'

It's Fowler three,
Don't kick the ball at me!
Van Nistlerooy dives,
Anelka gets another five.

Running past
The halfway line,
Oh dear!
It is now full-time.

Robbie Fowler
Is the hat-trick hero,
So United
Cheerio!

Chloe Statham (11)
Manchester Road Primary School

My Mum's Game

My mum's game,
Is put to shame.
It is called Ghost Master,
She couldn't play it any faster.
Her favourite is the Weather Witch,
On her arm is an enormous stitch.
Most of her favourites are banshees
She always uses, she's never he's
Now she completed 'Above the Cuckoo's Nest,'
Her wacky mind is laid to rest.

Rowanne Smalley (10)
Manchester Road Primary School

Games Day

It's the day today,
Time to go and play.

Play football,
Tennis,
Bat and ball,
Or be a menace.

Play cricket,
If you get a ticket.

Play lacrosse,
But don't go on the moss.

Play bat and ball,
And get the bat from the mall.

Play football,
But you can't be small.

You can clean the dishes,
Now you've finished.

Georgia Knott (10)
Manchester Road Primary School

My Life

My life is but a swirling mist
Upon a shelf in Death's domain,
Within its depths I seek
Every second of my life it leaks,
I seek for things that shall be found
In the future all these shall be unwound
Dropping away
The time I've filled
Until my life
Is finally spilled.

Michael Redman-Johnson (11)
Manchester Road Primary School

Ten Happy Puppies

Ten happy puppies
Eating lime
One got hyper
Then there were nine.

Nine happy puppies
Eating fish bait
One got reeled in
Then there were eight.

Eight happy puppies
Thinking of Heaven
One thought of Hell
Then there were seven.

Seven happy puppies
Playing magic tricks
One got turned into a hamster
Then there were six.

Six happy puppies
Learning the dolphin dive
One drowned
Then there were five.

Five happy puppies
Banging on the door
One got knocked out
Then there were four.

Four happy puppies
Teasing a bee
One got stung
Then there were three.

Three happy puppies
Sitting on the loo
One got flushed down
Then there were two.

Two happy puppies
Deactivating a bomb
One got blown up
Then there was one.

One happy puppy
Eating a bun
It was poison
Then there were none.

Aiden Smalley (9)
Manchester Road Primary School

Cats

Ten little cats all having fun, one went for an interview,
Lost track of time and then there were nine.

Nine little cats all playing out, one went off with a new mate
And then there were eight.

Eight little cats all went to Devon, one fell in love
And then there were seven.

Seven little cats all playing with sticks,
One got a splinter and then there were six.

Six little cats were alive, one had died
And then there were five.

Five little cats walking in a room, one walked into a door
And then there were four.

Four little cats climbing up a tree, one fell down
And then there were three.

Three little cats playing peek-a-boo, one got scared
And then there were two.

Two little cats looking at a swan, one got it
And then there was one.

One little cat all on its own, it had gone
And then there were none.

Toni Flynn (11)
Manchester Road Primary School

Animal Poem

Imagine a snake,
Thin as a cake.

Imagine a pig,
Doing a dig.

Imagine a dog,
Playing with a frog.

Imagine a flea,
Drinking tea.

Imagine a bear,
Sat in a chair.

Imagine a cat,
Wearing a hat.

Imagine a giraffe,
Having a laugh.

Imagine a seal,
Eating a meal.

Doha Salem (7)
Manchester Road Primary School

My Life The Giraffe

I am the giraffe, tall and confident,
Looking out for danger,
I go to the water hole looking carefully,
The other animals drinking,
Drip, drop, drip, drop,
Lion is off in the distance running towards me,
I panic, I run, I stop, he only wanted water.

I am the giraffe stretching my neck,
Up to the tallest leaf on the tree,
Crunch, crunch, crunch!

Jennifer Madeley (10)
Manchester Road Primary School

Animal Poem

Imagine a snake,
Thin as a cake.
Imagine a pig,
Wearing a wig.
Imagine a dog,
Having a jog.
Imagine a flea,
Eating me.
Imagine a bear,
With underwear.
Imagine a cat,
With a hat.
Imagine a giraffe,
Taking a bath.
Imagine a seal,
Having a meal.

Samuel Swinburn (7)
Manchester Road Primary School

My Crazy Family

My dad is sad
When United lose a match.

My mum has a chum
And her name is Sue.

My sister had a blister
When her shoes were too tight.

My nana has a bandanna
When she was dressed like a pirate.

My grandad had a shopping bag
When he went to Tesco.

And that's my crazy family!

Jake Moroney (10)
Manchester Road Primary School

Animal Poem

Imagine a snake,
Thin as a rake.

Imagine a pig,
Wearing a wig.

Imagine a dog,
In a fog.

Imagine a flea,
Making tea.

Imagine a bear,
Playing with hair.

Imagine a cat,
Playing with a rat.

Imagine a giraffe,
In the bath.

Imagine a seal,
Eating a meal.

Elliot Jones (8)
Manchester Road Primary School

Colours

Orange is the colour of my lunchbox,
Red is the colour of that fox,
Purple is the colour of my new lamp,
Pink is the colour of my stamp,
Brown is the colour of a chocolate bum,
Black is the colour of Adam's gun,
Yellow is the colour of Jade's bed,
Green is the colour of my dad's shed.

These are the colours I know.

Keely Maher (10)
Manchester Road Primary School

Animal Poem

Imagine a snake,
Thin as a rake.

Imagine a pig,
At a gig.

Imagine a dog,
Pushing a log.

Imagine a flea,
Eating a bee.

Imagine a bear,
In underwear.

Imagine a cat,
Having a chat.

Imagine a giraffe,
Playing maths.

Imagine a seal,
Having a meal.

Aron Bardsley (9)
Manchester Road Primary School

Cats, Cats Sleep Anywhere

(Based on 'Cats Sleepy Anywhere' by Eleanor Farjean)

Cats, cats sleep anywhere,
Up or down,
Or any chair,
In our beds,
Or in our sheds,
On the window,
Near the ledge,
Cats, cats sleep anywhere.

Rebecca Myerscough (9)
Manchester Road Primary School

Ten Little Frogs

Ten little frogs bouncing in a line
One hopped out, now there's nine.

Nine little frogs being used as bait
A shark ate one, now there's eight.

Eight little frogs bombing Devon
One bombed Hell, now there's seven.

Seven little frogs gathering sticks
One got scratched, now there's six.

Six little frogs all alive
One got shot, now there's five.

Five little frogs all felt sore
One got a cure, now there's four.

Four little frogs bashing a tree
One got crushed, now there's three.

Three little frogs drinking out of the loo
One got poisoned, now there's two.

Two little frogs circling the sun
One got dizzy, now there's one.

One frog all alone
He fell in water, now there's none.

Jakob Hitchen (9)
Manchester Road Primary School

Colours

Blue is the colour of City's kit,
Red is the colour of my big lips,
Green is the colour of my table pot,
Black is the colour of my bottle top,
Yellow is the colour of a sunflower,
Brown is the colour of a brick tower.

Sean Bradley (9)
Manchester Road Primary School

Colours!

Red is the colour of my red rose,
Red is the colour of a red, red rose.

Blue is the colour of the wonderful sky,
Blue is the colour of my blueberry pie.

Yellow is the colour of the golden sun,
Yellow is the colour of an iced bun.

Green is the colour of the swaying grass,
Green is the colour of a big green asp.

Purple is the colour of a bunch of grapes,
Purple is the colour of some people's gates.

Pink is the colour of our flesh,
Pink is the colour of some mesh.

Blake Marley & Olivia Sutcliffe (10)
Manchester Road Primary School

Mythical Creatures

Dragons breathing fire and flame,
Centaurs that are not so tame,
Harpies flying through the air,
Bigfoot coming from his lair,
Trolls eating human flesh,
Cyclops caged in wire mesh,
Mermaids with such a lovely voice,
Serpents in the lake so moist,
Unicorns with golden horns,
Vampires, though not many are born,
All these creatures are a con,
None of them are real not one!

Amy Ainsworth (9)
Manchester Road Primary School

My Future

What will be
Left here for me
When I grow up?

Will there be
Fish still swimming in the nice, clean water?
Will the animals survive the storms?

Will there be
Green grass to play sports on
And fresh food to eat?

Will there be
PlayStation 2s to play on?
Will there be Xboxes?

Will there be
Restaurants and
McDonald's?

Michael Tighe (9)
Manchester Road Primary School

My Future

What will be
Left here for me
When I grow up?

Will there be
Fruit to eat and
Horses and ponies left?

Will the water
Be fresh to drink
And animals to feed?

Will there be
Light and shine
When I grow up?

Lauren Campbell (9)
Manchester Road Primary School

My Future

What will be
Left here for me
When I grow up?

Will there be
Water to drink
And will it be clean?

Will there be
Electricity to play
Games and play on computers?

Will there be
Mums, dads and
Friends?

Will there be
Books to read
And to look at?

Will there be
Clothes to wear,
And to be able to swim?

Claire Wingfield (9)
Manchester Road Primary School

Football

Football is everything to me
Concentration is the key
Scoring goals and playing well
Who's the best? It's hard to tell
Making saves and controlling the defence
When a penalty is awarded the keeper becomes tense
Hitting the bar and hitting the post
They've hit the woodwork but they still came close
The game has ended - what a shame
It doesn't matter because I'll be coming again.

Matthew Winstanley (10)
Manchester Road Primary School

Football

I went to a City match
We only had ten men,
But on Sunday morning
We will have to start again
I watched the football
We scored another goal
But next time we play again
We will have to play at home.
Anelka got a penalty
He scored a great goal,
Then he ran around the pitch
And did a forward roll.
Boswell ran around the pitch
Passed the ball to Distin,
He lost control of the ball
And passed it to another man.
Fowler had the ball again
He kicked it in the net
Now my dad's got £80
Because he won the bet.
Next we played Liverpool
We scored at half-time,
But Tarnet hit the goalie post,
Cos he shot off from the line,
Macken ran down the pitch,
He ran like a storming foal,
He headed the ball
In the back of the net
And the commentator said, 'It's a goal!'

Chloe Woodcock (10)
Manchester Road Primary School

My Future

What will be
Left for me
When I grow up?

Will there be
Fresh air to breathe?
Will the sea be clean?

Will the rocks
Cover the parks?
Will they still be green?

Milk from goats,
Meat and veg
Will they still be fresh to eat?

Will the sunlight hurt?
Will the people on Earth
Be kind to animals?

Will dolphins play?
Will elephants and rhinos still survive?

Will you have left
Us anything
Healthy and living?

When I am older
And I'm the boss
What will it be worth,
If you have used
The goodness up
And destroyed all the Earth?

Danielle Whitehead (8)
Manchester Road Primary School

At The Bottom Of The Ocean

At the bottom of the ocean I can see . . .
Ten dancing dolphins playing like children,
Nine jumping jellyfish jumping like jelly babies,
Eight electric eels electrocuting like a socket,
Seven starfish sparkling like diamonds,
Six silly swordfish savaging like robbers,
Five freckly frogs jumping like kangaroos,
Four green sea turtles snapping like crocodiles,
Three grey sharks swaying like swans,
Two salamanders bathing lazily in the sun like a
Person on holiday,
One ginormous treasure chest sparkling like one huge diamond.

Rachel Hughes (8)
Manchester Road Primary School

At The Bottom Of The Ocean

At the bottom of the ocean I can see . . .
Ten shining starfish swimming like a child,
Nine splashing Nemos swaying like the breeze,
Eight bobbing mermaids bouncing like balls,
Seven sly frogs kicking like a football,
Six snapping sharks snapping the crocodiles,
Five silly sea horses jumping like kangaroos,
Four sharp swordfish fighting like knights,
Three shimmering goldfish shining like gold,
Two glittery treasure chests colourful like the rainbow,
One lonely ship with the name, Titanic.

Danielle Maguire (8)
Manchester Road Primary School

At The Bottom Of The Ocean

At the bottom of the ocean I can see . . .
Ten crunchy crabs crawling like spiders,
Nine naughty Nemos shooting round the ocean,
Eight snakes rolling like a roller coaster,
Seven scary sharks snapping like crocodiles,
Six funny frogs flexing like acrobats,
Five friendly fish swimming like turtles,
Four angry alligators gobbling up humans like sharks,
Three hammering hammerheads hammering like mad,
Two slimy eels smellier than pig muck,
One fat tortoise that fills up half of the ocean.

Jordan Lee Scattergood (9)
Manchester Road Primary School

At The Bottom Of The Ocean

At the bottom of the ocean I can see . . .
Ten tiny turtles flapping like birds,
Nine naughty Nemos striped like tiger sharks,
Eight electrical eels electrocuting like sockets,
Seven sets of seaweed swaying like the breeze
Six slimy sea snakes slithering like slugs,
Five fat frogs jumping like kangaroos,
Four hunting hammerheads spying like foxes,
Three threatening swordfish swimming like darts,
Two sly great whites killing fish like murderers,
One old treasure chest still shining like a diamond.

Chris Marsden (9)
Manchester Road Primary School

My Future

What will be
Left here for me
When I grow up?

Will there be
Cats and dogs
And water to drink?

Will there be
Fruit to eat
And sunny days?

Will there be
Cars and buses
And healthy food to eat?

Will there be
Air to breathe
And toys to play with?

Victoria Boardman (8)
Manchester Road Primary School

At The Bottom Of The Ocean

At the bottom of the ocean I can see . . .
Ten tiny turtles swimming like divers,
Nine naughty Nemos playing like a clown,
Eight enormous eels electrocuting like sockets,
Seven slimy water snakes rolling like a roller coaster,
Six scary sharks snapping like castanets,
Five funny frogs flexing like acrobats,
Four friendly fish flapping their fins like seals,
Three transparent tadpoles,
Two terrifying terrapins floating like starfish,
One huge octopus waving like people.

Amy Parkinson (9)
Manchester Road Primary School

My Future

What will be
Here for me
When I grow up?

Will there be
Oxygen from plants?
Will the air be clean?

Will there be
Animals roaming round?
Will the trees be green?

Will there be
Fresh food to eat?
Will it be clean to eat?

Will there be
Trees to give us shade?
Will there be flowers beneath our feet?

Holly Fox (9)
Manchester Road Primary School

I Wish I Could Be A Dolphin

I wish I could evolve into a dolphin,
I could glide through the sea,
I could swim and be free,
Oh I wish I could be a dolphin.

Oh I wish I could be a dolphin,
In my skin, so sleek and blue,
I could have the same soul too,
Oh I wish I could be a dolphin.

Sarah Yates (10)
Manchester Road Primary School

Colours

Blue is the colour of City's home ground,
Red is the colour of a rose,
Purple is the colour of my bedroom,
Yellow is the colour of a sunflower,
Bronze is the colour of a penny,
Gold is the colour of a one pound coin,
Silver is the colour of my mum's car,
Pink is the colour of my T-shirt,
White is the colour of a piece of paper,
Burberry is the colour of my handbag
Green is the colour of grass
Black is the colour of my PS2,
Grey is the colour of the sky,
Peach is the colour of our walls inside our classroom.

Tessa Herrington (10)
Manchester Road Primary School

My Cat!

My cat is fat
But he does not eat rats
He smells like a teddy
But isn't as fluffy
Except for his big fat tummy
He purrs when I scratch his ears
But he growls when I howl
He can't bounce
Be he can pounce
My cat likes to play but not in the day
You can't buy him today
Or you'll be throwing your money away.

Kelsea Mullen (10)
Manchester Road Primary School

My Cat

My cat Jessy
Can be very messy,
Her fur is black and white
And she sometimes stays out all night.

Her eyes are green
And she is very keen
She is three
And loves to sit on my knee.

She is a very clean cat
And she loves to lie on her mat
She likes to play with her toy mouse
And always runs about the house.

Sophie Morris (11)
Manchester Road Primary School

Monkeys

Monkeys are brown
They never have a frown
Then sometimes they moan
When they get out of bed, they wear a gown,
Monkeys swing and climb up trees
And sometimes feel the breeze,
Then they freeze
Or sometimes feel the squeeze
Monkeys whizzing up trees and doing a dance
While wearing pants
They're always eating ants.

Ben Burslam (10)
Manchester Road Primary School

My Future

What will be
There for me
When I grow up?
Will there be
Oxygen from plants?
Will the air be clean?
Will there be
Animals roaming around?
Will the trees be green?
Will there be
Fresh food to eat?
Will it be clean to eat?
Will there be
Trees to give us shade?
Will there be flowers under our feet?

Harry Blackwell (8)
Manchester Road Primary School

At The Bottom Of The Ocean

At the bottom of the ocean I can see . . .
Ten shimmering sea horses bobbing like balls,
Nine glittery goldfish gleaming like diamonds,
Eight bunches of swaying seaweed swaying like swans,
Seven slim mermaids swimming like a gentle princess,
Six snappy sharks snapping like castanets,
Five furious octopuses flexible like a gymnast,
Four funny frogs croaking like people with a sore throat,
Three sparkling blowfish shining like gold,
Two jumping jellyfish stinging like bees,
One glittery treasure chest shining like stars.

Bethany Waite (8)
Manchester Road Primary School

At The Bottom Of The Ocean

At the bottom of the ocean I can see . . .
Ten snappy swordfish fighting like knights,
Nine electrical eels flashing like a loose socket,
Eight silly clownfish acting like a bunch of clowns,
Seven graceful starfish spinning like spiralling tops,
Six pink jellyfish bouncing like balls,
Four leaping dolphins playing like children,
Three crunchy crabs crunchy like a Crunchie bar,
Two big whales grunting like pigs,
One orange octopus waving his arms.

Bethany Parry (8)
Manchester Road Primary School

The Writer Of This Poem
(Based on 'The Writer Of This Poem' by Roger McGough)

The writer of this poem . . .
Is as giddy as a jester,
As wild as a madman,
As hilarious as Jasper Carrott,
As tricky to work out as an English test,
As aggressive as George Bush,
As rational as Tony Blair,
(It's great what the poem says!)

The writer of this poem . . .
Is as sensible as a spider,
As clever as Frankenstein,
As yappy as a dog,
As quick as an athlete,
As polite as your mum,
As mischievous as a monkey,
As fine as a cloth,
As elegant as the Queen,
(It's getting better and better.)

Ben Ashmore (8)
Moorside Primary School

The Writer Of This Poem
Based on 'The Writer Of This Poem' by Roger McGough)

The writer of this poem is . . .
As fit as a fiddle and also very cute,
As strong as a bodybuilder lifting weights,
As gentle as a cat sleeping peacefully.

As fast as a cheetah chasing its prey,
As slow as the tortoise racing the hare,
As happy as a juggler making people laugh,
As silly as a clown at the circus.

As fashionable as Britney Spears,
As tall as a tree,
As sporty as a football player,
And as fussy as can be.

Victoria Shaw (9)
Moorside Primary School

School

School is sometimes really cool
But there are so many rules,
No sweets to eat, no chewing gum
Apart from that it's really fun!

Kacie Andrew (7)
Moorside Primary School

Santa, Elves And Me!

On Santa's sleigh you see the snow,
I wonder if he does not know
That I am good and he is bad,
I've never seen his elves so sad.

Rachel Parkinson (8)
Moorside Primary School

The Writer Of This Poem
(Based on 'The Writer Of This Poem' by Roger McGough)

The writer of this poem is Nathan,
He is taller than Big Ben,
As strong as a rhinoceros charging at a tree,
As gentle as a black and white cat.

As fast as a cheetah catching its prey,
As slow as a slug getting home,
As happy as a clown doing jokes,
As silly as a hyena laughing at a giraffe.

As sporty as a football player,
As dangerous as a hunter hunting,
Hair as short as grass in the garden,
As fat as a pink piglet.

Nathan Gee (8)
Moorside Primary School

What Is Colour Like?

I asked the little boy who cannot see,
'What is colour like?'
Blue is like raindrops falling from the sky,
Pink is like the sudden softness of a pillow,
Yellow is like a little chick that has just been born,
Purple is like a boiled sweet when you crunch it,
Red is like a trumpet sound of burning cheeks,
Black is like darkness in a night sky,
Orange is like a tropical sunset,
Brown is like chocolate and cola,
Ready to be drunk and eaten.

Charlotte Carr (9)
Moorside Primary School

The Writer Of This Poem
(Based on 'The Writer of this Poem' by Roger McGough)

The writer of this poem is . . .
As sporty as a footballer playing in a match,
As strong as a bodybuilder at his work,
As gentle as a cat sleeping on a window sill,
As fast as Paula Radcliffe running on a track,
As slow as a tortoise racing a hare,
As happy as a clown performing in front of children,
As silly as a worm going in water,
As brave as a boxing glove punching someone,
As tall as a tree,
As thin as a piece of paper,
As chatty as a chatterbox.

Kerrianne Maloney (9)
Moorside Primary School

The Writer Of This Poem
(Based on 'The Writer of this Poem' by Roger McGough)

The writer of this poem is smaller than an ant,
As strong as a big hairy bear who eats you,
As gentle as a feather that falls down,
As fast as an Olympic runner,
As slow as a snail that slithers on the ground,
As happy as a teacher who marks good boy's work,
As silly as a clown who tells funny jokes,
As hot as fire that burns through the night,
As fit as a footballer who scores a goal,
As musical as a pop star who sings with the angels,
As nice and loving as a heart that pumps in your body.

Dylan Yates (9)
Moorside Primary School

The Writer Of This Poem
(Based on 'The Writer Of This Poem' by Roger McGough)

The writer of this poem is Holly Jones,
As strong as a plane floating in space,
As gentle as a pencil smooth and soft,
As fast as a hare running as fast as she can,
As slow as a tortoise eating juicy grass,
As happy as a sunset going down slowly,
As silly as a crow singing a song,
As clever as a fox thinking of an idea,
As cheeky as a monkey pinching a banana,
As fancy as a wedding day, or
Someone who has won the lottery,
As fierce as a bear getting its prey.

Holly Jones (8)
Moorside Primary School

I Asked A Girl Who Could Not See

What is colour like?

Blue is like the wavy sea swishing from side to side,
Pink is like a calm bunch of roses sitting on the ground,
White is like a smooth piece of paper lying on the desk,
Green is like smooth silk waiting to be worn,
Red is like bumpy strawberries sitting in the fridge,
Yellow is like bright stars twinkling in the night sky,
Yellow is like a newborn chick lying next to its mother,
Pink is like your wrinkly skin when you are sitting in the bath,
White is like a clean shirt in the wash and
Blue is like slippery ice covering the streams.

Leanne Marie Sandbach (9)
Moorside Primary School

The Writer Of This Poem
(Based on 'The Writer Of This Poem' by Roger McGough)

The writer of this poem is . . .
As cheeky as someone's dimples;
As lazy as a tabby cat;

As tiny as a baby ant;
As kind as a grandma;
As loving as a cute puppy;

As scary as a black bat;
As dopey as a white dormouse;
As funny as Peter Kay!

Samantha Clarke (9)
Moorside Primary School

I Asked The Little Boy Who Cannot See

What is colour like?
Blue is like the sea, the big cold sea,
Pink is quiet like the sunset sky, or petals,
Yellow is quite, calm and plain, like stars of buttercups,
Green is bold, bold and cold, like hills or leaves,
Red is angry, wacky and bold, like the Devil's telling me to
                                do B-A-D, *bad,*
White is cooling, like a limo going to Pop Idol in the snow.

Daniel Pitman (9)
Moorside Primary School

I Asked The Little Boy Who Cannot See

What is colour like?
Blue is like the calm lake flowing through the trees,
Yellow is like the sign of spring when baby chicks are born.
White is like silence running through the room,
Pink is like the soft petals falling gently to the ground.
Red is like a lightning bolt because it is so *bold.*

Jessica Phillips (9)
Moorside Primary School

The Writer Of This Poem
(Based on 'The Writer Of This Poem' by Roger McGough)

The writer of this poem is . . .
As strong as an elephant,
As gentle as a flower,
As fast as the wind,
As slow as a space walker,
As happy as the sun,
As silly as a chicken,
As clever as a computer.

Zachary M A Smith (9)
Moorside Primary School

Cats Of The Week

Monday's cat is far too fat,
Tuesday's cat sits on the mat,
Wednesday's cat saw some dogs,
Thursday's cat climbed some logs,
Friday's cat played 'tig' with me,
Saturday's cat played a trick on Paul Klee,
Sunday's cat eats his meat
In one gollop, then falls in a heap.

Chris Kinsey (9)
Moorside Primary School

I Asked The Little Girl Who Cannot See

What is colour like?
Blue is like frozen ice waiting to be cracked,
Green is like the hills whistling proud and high,
Red is like fresh strawberries in the brown basket,
White is like the slushy snow melting every second,
Pink is like calm flower petals falling off the pollen
And lilac is like smooth clouds coming my way!

Charlotte Orton (9)
Moorside Primary School

I Asked A Boy Who Cannot See

What is colour like?

Blue is like the lake swaying to and fro,
Red is like the sunset in the dusk of night,
Pink is like candyfloss melting in your mouth,
Yellow is like dandelions brightening up the day,
White is like lightning flashing in the sky,
Black is like the sky scaring you at night,
Purple is like a lollipop with a tempting taste.

Sophie Woods (9)
Moorside Primary School

I Asked The Boy Who Couldn't See

What is colour like?

White is like the snow pouring from the sky,
Yellow is like the sun melting the snow,
Blue is like the clear blue sky,
Green is like a new rose stem,
Pink is like sweet tulips on the green, green grass,
Red is like a sore nose
And pink is like rosy-red cheeks.

Rebecca Ellis (8)
Moorside Primary School

A Cat Week

Monday's cat is as flat as a mat,
Tuesday's cat is so fat,
Wednesday's cat has so much joy,
Thursday's cat has an owner called Roy,
Friday's cat goes out at night,
Saturday's cat is so bright,
Sunday's cat is a handful.

Thomas Pratt (8)
Moorside Primary School

I Asked The Little Boy Who Cannot See

I asked the little boy who cannot see,
What is colour like?
Pink is like the sunset sky going back to is peaceful sleep,
Yellow is like the dazzling sun that attracts your eyes,
Blue is like skidding ice and the frozen leaves,
Red is like a devil with fangs and sharp horns,
White is like the snow that falls gently onto the ground,
Pink is like candyfloss that melts in your mouth,
Yellow is like a dandelion lying on the peaceful earth,
Blue is like sea swishing away,
Red is like a bunch of roses being picked,
White is like a stretched limo going to the awards.

Thomas Bullock (9)
Moorside Primary School

The Writer Of This Poem
(Based on 'The Writer Of This Poem' by Roger McGough)

The writer of this poem is . . .
Cameron,
As strong as the iron man lifting a school,
As gentle as a puppy that's just been born,
As fast as a cheetah running through the forest,
As slow as a tortoise plodding on the path,
As happy as a millionaire winning his money,
As silly as a clown doing his show,
As small as an ant eating a piece of grass,
As big as an elephant stamping in the wild.

Cameron Conley (8)
Moorside Primary School

I Asked The Little Boy Who Cannot See, The Writer Of This Poem
(Based on 'The Writer Of This Poem' by Roger McGough)

The writer of this poem is Jodie Holden,
As strong as the Great Wall that is built in China,
As gentle as a chick breaking out of its egg,
As fast as a cheetah running through the grass,
As slow as a tortoise plodding along the path,
As happy as a juggler juggling seven balls,
As silly as a circus clown riding a one-wheeled bike,
As kind as my dad giving me money,
As pretty as Cinderella at the ball,
As beautiful as Princess Fiona and Sleeping Beauty dancing,
As cheeky as a monkey swinging through the trees.

Jodie Holden (8)
Moorside Primary School

What Is Colour Like?

Green is like leaves swaying on the tree,
Red is like a danger sign shouting *stop!*
Blue is like the sky drifting slowly, going nowhere,
Pink is calm and bubbly like a fluffy cloud,
Orange is like a burning fire spreading fast,
Yellow is like a dandelion telling us it's spring,
Purple is a crashing and bashing thunderstorm,
Brown is like the rough bark on a lonely tree,
And white is like a dream that you never want to end.

Jack Henshaw (8)
Moorside Primary School

Cats Of The Week

Monday's cat has a big, fat belly,
Tuesday's cat scoffs lots of jelly,
Wednesday's cat plays with balls of yarn,
Thursday's cat lives on a farm,
Friday's cat has bright ginger fur,
Saturday's cat causes up a stir,
Sunday's cat is always lazy,
Super, mad and very crazy.

Chelsie O'Keeffe (9)
Moorside Primary School

Sharks

You're lying on the dark blue waves,
It's such a lovely day,
You see a fin in the water
And it's coming your way!
You swim to the shore,
Or become a person pie,
If you don't want to be a snack,
I think you had better go back!

April Stanhope (8)
Moorside Primary School

Who Is She?

Who is she, standing there
In the cold and frosty air?
Who is she, sitting on the floor
By the warm and cosy doorstep of her house?
Who is she, standing in the cold on the beach?

Hannah Starkie (8)
Moorside Primary School

Hearts

Hearts flatter everywhere,
People say 'Look over there,
They are shiny and bright,
They're a lovely sight.'
They are cool to some,
Especially my mum,
Hearts are so bright,
They glisten in the night.

Letifah Dervan (10)
Rolls Crescent Primary School

My Visit To The Hospital

I sat in the waiting room,
My heart beat like giant's feet,
The nurse shouted me in.

The nurse looked at my foot,
'This won't hurt!'
Said the nurse, like I was a baby.

I went back to the waiting room,
Waiting for the doctor,
He shouted us in,
That's when I got worried.

I could see instruments,
The doctor came in,
He had it in his hand.

My mum stayed with me,
She held my hand
And the doctor said, 'I will put antiseptic on.'

I could see lots of horrible things,
People crying and screaming,
I could feel the wood being eased out.

Lauren Grimshaw (9)
St Mary's CE Primary School, Davyhulme

A Day At My New School

I stepped out of my car and walked through the gates,
'Bye Mum and Dad.'
Then ran to see the big playground.

I felt scared but excited,
Frightened but happy,
Everyone welcomed me with open arms.

Children kept on asking my name,
Like a broken record,
I now felt happy that people wanted to know me,
I was so thrilled.

I saw a teacher displaying some work,
And some others chattered,
As children played, they all pointed at me.

I walked into the school,
Then stamped my foot,
It echoed like hollow wood.

I heard the telephones and the voices,
Loud voices sounded like a giant's laugh,
The whistle blew, I was lost already.

Shelby Reavy (10)
St Mary's CE Primary School, Davyhulme

The Kingfisher

The kingfisher is an
Unusual bird
If you see one, you'll have to observe,
They have coloured feathers from birth
I bet you'll never see one surf.

Kingfishers are great so don't be late,
If you're going to see one,
Good luck because they're nearly all gone.

Amy Hall (8)
St Mary's CE Primary School, Davyhulme

Magical Hospital

Suddenly I got rushed into a huge hospital,
With many people in it,
I heard in my head, lots of screaming.

They started getting all the tools out,
My mum was allowed to stay in,
Trouser legs pulled up ready for the X-ray.

They gave my mum magic medicine,
Two spoonfuls a day to make my legs better,
I could walk in a few days time.

I went back home from there,
More magical medicine for me,
It was nice, I only had it for two weeks.

No more medicine for me,
I could walk but not quite right,
I went back in again to see if I was better.

I could walk properly again,
Run about and play games,
At last, call for my friends.

Joe Cooper (10)
St Mary's CE Primary School, Davyhulme

The Puffin

The puffin is very hard to find,
You see it and keep it in your mind,
You cannot spell it but you'll have to learn,
You'll wait and wait till it's your turn,
The puffin bird is hard to find,
You could see two, you could see nine,
This puffin has a coloured beak,
His little legs won't make him weak,
The puffin is very hard to find,
You see it and keep it in your mind.

Emily Hall (8)
St Mary's CE Primary School, Davyhulme

I'm Scared Of Injections

I sat down in the waiting room,
Scared that something would happen,
Suddenly I was shaking like big jellies.

'Ready for you now,' called the doctor,
My heart felt like it was going to stop,
I thought that I would never wake up.

I walked in the little room,
My skin was full of goosebumps,
Like I felt as if I was going to be sick.

Then on the bed with a pillow, I lay
The doctor turned my head,
The injection went in with a scream.

Hours later I woke up from a long sleep,
Rubber gloves were like plastic bands,
Children were screaming in my head.

The room next door to me had instruments,
Injection lids falling off, I didn't know what to do!
Parents I heard being happy, just like mine.

Alicia McGrath (9)
St Mary's CE Primary School, Davyhulme

The Animals In The Zoo

The animals in the zoo are in lots of different places,
There are lots of zebras in the zoo,
There are lots of bears, snakes, tigers, lions,
Lizards, armadillos, anteaters, snakes, fish,
Crocodiles, elephants, monkeys, penguins,
Sealions, sharks, kangaroos, bison, buffalo,
Puma, lama, antelope, frogs, turtles and camels.

The zoo is fantastic and it is fun,
We run to all the animals,
The animals are great.

Sam Robertshaw (7)
St Mary's CE Primary School, Davyhulme

A Trip To The City Of Manchester Stadium

I was very excited,
It was like all of England
Were squeezed into seats,
It was exciting but frightening.

The spiral steps were killing me,
The programmes were £1.50, same as usual,
It was big but tiny.

It did not feel the same as Maine Road,
Fans called it the Blue Camp, the game began,
Ten minutes later, 2 down, crowd went silent.

Half-time whistle went,
Fans got burgers and chips,
Bang! Bang! Bang! The seats go.

The smell of the food is overwhelming,
The whistle goes,
The fans come back.

Fans singing Blue Moon and MCFC,
Sibierski scored,
The crowd went wild.

Alex Platt (10)
St Mary's CE Primary School, Davyhulme

Busted

My favourite band is Busted,
They rock until they drop,
My favourite band is Busted,
Can't help it, they're just top!

Now Charlie is my favourite
And he's got the best voice,
The other two are pretty good,
But my favourite one to tell the truth,
Has got to be . . . Charlie.

Lucy Pickering (9)
St Mary's CE Primary School, Davyhulme

A Is For Astronaut

A is for astronaut flying through space,
B is for bird singing a song,
C is for car in a race,
D is for duck with a neck so long,
E is for eel swimming in the sea,
F is for friends just you and me,
G is for gear just the size for you,
H is for hat you wear it on your head,
I is for ink, a lovely dark blue
J is for jam, a sticky substance on bread,
K is for Kale, a green little leaf,
L is for lips, so we can say, 'Good grief,'
M is for morning rise and shine,
N is for naked, when you're drunk with wine,
O is for owls, hooting at night,
P is for pills, to set you right,
Q is for queen, the one with the crown,
R is for road, the road into town,
S is for snakes, slithering along the ground,
T is for tambourine, jingly and round,
U is for unicorn with a golden horn,
V is for van selling all its corn,
W is for wind blowing every person's hair,
X is for excitement that's rare,
Y is for you because you've got a mare,
Z is for zero, oh it's time to go.

Martin Wood (8)
St Mary's CE Primary School, Davyhulme

The Dog Called Blue

There was a dog called Blue,
Who swallowed a bottle of glue,
He started to choke,
So someone gave him a poke
And he did a gluey poo!

Oliver Rothwell (8)
St Mary's CE Primary School, Davyhulme

Goodbye Tonsils

I could hear the sirens of the ambulance,
As I went through the sliding doors,
Injured people cluttered the waiting room.

My throat had had its last day with its tonsils,
My heart beat faster than a cheetah,
'We're ready now' said the nurse.

The doctor slowly injected the anaesthetic,
I soon drifted to a dreamy world,
I remembered nothing else until I woke up.

'Wakey, wakey' whispered the doctor,
Everything was a blur of colours, like a rainbow,
My throat felt like it was strangled but much better.

The trolleys clattered down the corridor,
I was a subdued mouse,
Machines beeped throughout the hospital.

I felt sick but hungry,
My tummy was rumbling like a purring cat,
I don't know why I was dreading such a thing.

Sarah Marland (10)
St Mary's CE Primary School, Davyhulme

I Wish

I wish I had a motorbike that roared loudly.
I wish I had a computer so I could play games.
I wish I had a park just for me.
I wish I had a mansion.
I wish I had a dog that I could play with.
I wish I had a friend that I could play with every day.
I wish I had a fridge that had food in all the time.
I wish all my wishes could come true.

James Wilson-Jevon (8)
St Mary's CE Primary School, Davyhulme

Brace Or No Brace?

The warmth of the waiting room made me feel sick and hot,
All I could think was brace or no brace?
The receptionist reassured me, but I was still worried.

When the assistant came through, I knew it was time,
I felt as scared as a mouse, I stood up with my family,
My mum waited while I sank into the purple chair.

The masked man peered over me, checking my teeth,
Then the nurse took me into a room,
I had to bite a pad while a box bleeped circling my head.

Tube forced into my mouth whilst in the purple chair room,
I was forced to look at weird pictures,
I just wanted to go home.

The door squeaked open,
I felt like a wild stallion freed from hunters galloping away,
But I dreaded the next time.

Jessica Walker (9)
St Mary's CE Primary School, Davyhulme

The Every-Animal-You-Could-Think-Of Shop

Every day the women from the shop said, 'Time to go.'
The badger from the basement said, 'Ho, ho, ho!'
'Don't say that,' said the armadillo.
Next the crocodile said, 'What's all the noise?'
Then the monkeys had woken up and thrown all of their toys!
Then the cat turned back and hadn't got a clue!
Then the grizzly bear said, 'Boo!'
Next the seal was on a wheel and said, 'What's the big deal?'
The eel on the other eels said, 'We just love wheels.'
The panda liked the tango and made a mocking smile.
The tapir could not get out of the tiles to build his piles.
'I'm sure the lady will come back another while.'

Alicia Buckley (7)
St Mary's CE Primary School, Davyhulme

Mummy

Ding dong - 'Next please,'
My turn, the wait ended,
Would it be amputated?

'See the doctor' said the nurse,
I went to the children's place,
He looked at me and said,

'Go to get it X-rayed,'
Looking at lots of signs and doors to get there,
Shhflulsh went the box.

To the plaster room now,
Through slamming doors, passed squeaking trolleys,
My ankle had been mummified.

As I limped out of the dome of doom,
I heard children crying as they were parted,
Like the Red Sea, from their family.

Never again, not a place to go with a headache,
I walked like a drunk,
I was a tramp.

Sophie Irving (9)
St Mary's CE Primary School, Davyhulme

I Like Books

I like books that are interesting to read
I like stories that are funny indeed
I like information books reading in a shed
I like books reading on a coach
I like joke books that are quite funny
I like story books with some lines that are funny
I like school books that are interesting to read
I like books that tell you what to build.

Luke May (8)
St Mary's CE Primary School, Davyhulme

Princess' Palace

Once there lived a princess,
Who had a little maid,
A very kind princess,
A very evil maid!
The princess had a pink dress,
The maid had a frown.
The day the princess saw the maid
She was looking down.
The princess tried to reassure her,
But still she was looking down,
The maid was working a plan,
Soon it was spick and span.
The princess was amazed to find herself in a tower,
She looked down her window even lower,
There down below her stood a prince,
He gazed at her dreamily as she called to him
And he took her away before you could say sim!

Koel Raychaudhuri (8)
St Mary's CE Primary School, Davyhulme

Autumn Time

Twirly, whirly autumn is coming,
Scary night, spooky night, trick and treat night,
Whirly, curly leaves are twisting and twirling down,
Oak tree waving down the path,
Oak tree waving down the path,
Dirty birds flying away,
Early birds coming here,
Naughty tree letting leaves go!
Let's go trick and treating,
Let's go trick and treating,
Let's twirl the leaves around,
Over the bush, there is a party of
Whirling leaves, twirling, whirling leaves,
Curling leaves making a hurry burry cane.

Matthew Marshall (7)
St Mary's CE Primary School, Davyhulme

Fix My Teeth . . . Please

As I was waiting for the operating theatre,
all I could hear was my heart pounding.
Fear was running through my veins.

'Amelia, we are ready for you,' said the doctor.
I couldn't do it, so I started screaming.
Suddenly I was . . . asleep.

I woke up very slowly,
all I could see was a white light.
I turned my head but everything was blurred.

'Are you alright?' asked my mum.
She rushed to see me like an over protective animal.
I didn't want all this fuss, I was exhausted.

Bleep, bleep, went the heart machine annoyingly.
My teeth and gums were feathers.
So delicate and gentle.

I didn't think my teeth were better
but they were, I could eat.
Wow, was I relieved!

Amelia Scott-Steele (9)
St Mary's CE Primary School, Davyhulme

Litter

I look on the floor, litter everywhere.
Nowhere to have our picnic.
Take the things out of the basket,
Litter is everywhere.
Mum, there's a bin there
To throw litter, it is bad
Why do people do it?
It makes the world look messy
I wish one day it will stop
And I bet it will, don't you?

Lorna Riley (7)
St Mary's CE Primary School, Davyhulme

My First Visit To Old Trafford

I got out of my car,
Walking towards the Theatre of Dreams.
Amazing smell came from the ground.

There were millions of people outside.
Strangers were giving their tickets
Clunk, clink, kerching.

We walked into the ground.
A sea of aisles and steps.
A small beam of light came from a tunnel.

I wobbled through the tunnel, it was amazing.
Light shone like gold in the sun.
The ground was shaking like an earthquake.

The match began, the crowd suddenly roared.
Singing and shouting for England.
We scored, a deafening roar began.

Half-time approached, I smelt food.
The match began again, no one was there?
People came flooding in like water in a hole of a lifeboat.

Joe Murphy (9)
St Mary's CE Primary School, Davyhulme

There Was A Boy Called Sam

There was a boy called Sam
Who was brought up in West Ham.
He ate a large juicy peach
And turned into a leech
And got squashed by his auntie Pam.

Sam Gilmour (8)
St Mary's CE Primary School, Davyhulme

Hospital Trip

My arm was angry.
I saw buildings and it was big.
It was full of injured people.

The place was loud and noisy.
When the door opened mobiles bleeped.
A cold breeze fell upon me.

I was a bit lonely
The doors swung open
And the lift bleeped.

My arm was freezing off the anaesthetic
I was scared because of the moaning patients.
My arm was paralysed.

There was only fruit to eat.
The nurses started to leave.
It was dark outside.

The machines started to beep.
The people chatted.
The anaesthetic wore off and my arm felt better.

Jordan Southern (9)
St Mary's CE Primary School, Davyhulme

There Was A Dog On A Mat

There was a dog on a mat
Who wore a silly green hat
He chased a mouse
Into a house
He ran into a wall and went splat!

Luke Woolstencroft (9)
St Mary's CE Primary School, Davyhulme

The Invisible Man And The Puppy

Listen to him he's talking to me,
He knew I had it.
I ran, ran, ran, ran, but I didn't know where he was,
He kicked me but I had it.
He kicked me but I had it.
I found something on the ground,
It was money then it flew up in the air.
I ran, ran, ran, ran, but I didn't know where he was.
He kicked me but I had it.
He kicked me but I had it.
I tried to get to school,
I saw things floating in the air.
I ran, ran, ran, ran, but I didn't know where he was.
He kicked me but I had it.
He kicked me but I had it.
When I got to school I heard a scream,
Then the whistle blew.
I ran, ran, ran, ran, but I didn't know where he was.
He kicked me but I had it.
He kicked me but I had it.
He kicked me and I dropped it.
Oh no!

Eleanor Wright (7)
St Mary's CE Primary School, Davyhulme

Untitled

When I got in the car
my mum said, 'Are you ready to go?'
It felt weird going to a new house.

When the car was going past the houses
I saw children playing.
I got there.

As I got out of the car
people were looking out of their windows
smiling at me.

When I walked in the house
I was getting worried
I was getting tears in my eyes.

I stepped on the floor
it started to creek
when I stepped on the floor.

We looked through the window
looking at the squirrels
eating the nuts in my new garden.

Courtney Edge (9)
St Mary's CE Primary School, Davyhulme

Thomas In The Big Blue Stadium

The huge building was new to me,
blue tops were a brilliant sea,
tip tap of the footsteps created a beat.

Apprehension was passing away,
excitement was a flower growing,
new faces were a museum full of art.

The chairs were flapping like birds,
it was joyful.
Drinks were drank with a great slurp.

Chants were sung all around,
it was raucous like everyone was talking to me.
As they sang, their voices were one.

The intensity grew
fantastic feelings exploded.
Goal! or crescendo of 'Yes!' erupted from the crowd.

I was so happy
it was a home away from home.
We felt like a big family.

Thomas Radcliffe (10)
St Mary's CE Primary School, Davyhulme

Holiday

The plane cool and calm but bumpy.
We stood on the ground again safe and sound.
A city sat on the coast.

The beach was like the sun.
Whilst the heat hit me like a bullet.
The night moved on.

The party's stopped.
The night slept.
The morning woke.

The shells on the beach were like an art gallery.
The city soundless, not deafening.
The seagulls screeched like gorgons.

The wind sailed round the land like a ship.
Warm and cool, strong and weak.
Tides started to grow like a new seed.

The unusual voices I heard were from strangers.
It got stranger and stranger.
It was like they were talking to me!

Alex Jones (9)
St Mary's CE Primary School, Davyhulme

My Worst Fear

Lots of nurses wiping up blood.
People being ill, lying in bed.
People saying I'm in pain and agony.

Waiting in rooms children screaming.
I don't want to go in.
I got to the room, all I could hear was just a prick.

All I could feel was the needle pricking me.
Blood trickling down me.
I was sick and white as a ghost.

All that nerve was just for nothing.
As soon as I got out of the place
Everyone said, 'Are you OK?'

As soon as I squeezed blood came out.
It started tipping out of the cut.
I took off the plaster to have a look.

My mum started to worry.
More paper towels to wipe up the blood.
At last, home, I jumped into bed.

Rebecca Simister (9)
St Mary's CE Primary School, Davyhulme

My Teeth Problem

The building had lots of people inside,
Lots of rooms and passages.
People started and pointed at my mum and me.

The nurse told me to go into this passageway,
The room of doom came upon me,
It was frightening and I started to cry.

A large x-ray machine sat in that room,
I put my teeth on this yellow torch.
That was it, all done.

I came out of the building
My teeth felt very different, very dry,
I really wanted a drink but I was not allowed.

It felt like I had a horrible drink that stuck in my throat,
My teeth squeaked like they were brand new.
The cool breeze made my teeth shiver.

Hours later I had a drink,
My teeth were cool again.
No! My ears hurt now.

Helen Lyons (10)
St Mary's CE Primary School, Davyhulme

My Worst Hospital Visit

I was waiting in a chair,
My head felt like it was going to explode
My mum came, no stitches!

As I waited, a patient was rushed past
It scared me stiff,
I thought that my head wasn't there.

Suddenly, the nurse called my name,
Lots of masked people were staring at me,
I felt as sick as a dog.

As I opened my eyes, everything was blurry,
There was bleeping noises.
My mum was there, she said, 'Are you OK?'

My head was a raging bull,
There was a clanking and a clunking, I wanted to get out
I was like an eagle escaping an attack.

I went out and my trousers crackled,
The cold grabbed me as I went out,
It was good to get out.

Peter Dawson (9)
St Mary's CE Primary School, Davyhulme

The Monster

It's blackish-grey following me
I asked nobody to come for tea
It's copying me and it won't stop
Even when I go to the shop!
I can't wait for winter when it's dark
For that is better than summer in the park
The things that fear me most are these monsters
They fear me more than lobsters!
At last I thought I had to speak up
Even if my mum doesn't give me good luck.
I said to him, 'Look you silly monster shape,
You're not stickier than sticky tape.
So stop following me
Because I didn't invite you to tea.'
My mum told me while she was kneading some dough
'It's only your own shadow.'
I said, she was wrong
But then something donged
And told me she was right!

Rhea Leslie (8)
St Mary's CE Primary School, Davyhulme

When You Are In Bed

When you are in bed tucked up tight
Do you have a fear something will give you a fright?
Under your bed in the wardrobe
Even in bed tucked up with you!
Dark purple fur as sleek as a cat
Yellow unbrushed sharp teeth as yellow as the sun.
Claws as sharp as a tiger's
Horns of a bull
Coming up the stairs to get you,
Opens your door and it's just your mum.
But what if it isn't your mum or dad?

Liam Magrath (8)
St Thomas More RC Primary School, Middleton

Days Of The Week

Monday, Monday
Boring work day.

Tuesday, Tuesday
It's just a flu day.

Wednesday, Wednesday
Is a messy day.

Thursday, Thursday
A really hard learning day.

Friday, Friday
It's a deciding day.

Saturday, Saturday
Just a clatter day.

Sunday, Sunday
It's a fun day.

Hooray!

Laura Hankinson (8)
St Thomas More RC Primary School, Middleton

Funny Poem

One windy December afternoon
When the grass was dancing
The birds were shouting
The sun lay on the ground.
I went in my house to get a drink
But I cooked an apple in the oven,
I went outside again and played baseball,
When it was my turn to bat I hit a boy.
When it was 10 o'clock at night
I was reading the news.
I went to get dressed
I hope nobody saw me.
I had to go to bed.

Jordan Lazenbury (8)
St Thomas More RC Primary School, Middleton

Spring

It will be spring soon
I could jump to the moon.

The flowers are in bloom
You splash about in a paddling pool.

Animals are born
Baby bulls grow a horn.

The grass is green
It looks clean.

You eat Easter eggs
And exercise your legs.

You go on holiday
Far far away.

You go walking up a hill
It's a thrill.

The seas are blue
Now, what does spring mean to you?

Harley McIntosh (8)
St Thomas More RC Primary School, Middleton

Opposites Poem

The sun is on the ground shaped like a hill
The hills are in the sky
Falling to the ground.
The wind is getting blown away
And the leaves are staying still.
The flowers are flying in the sky
And the birds are getting petals.

Rhiannon Prestage (8)
St Thomas More RC Primary School, Middleton

School Day

7am, *Ding ding!* another day
After school it's time to play
Pull on a uniform, wash the face
Eat my cornflakes, pack the bag
Race to school, don't break a rule
And off goes the bell.

9am, hang up my coat
And go to class,
Arithmetic is next,
Hurry, hurry, get my snack.
Breaktime already?
Hooray, hooray!

Next it's lunch, urgh! gross,
I think I'm going to throw up *bleeech!*
'Call the nurse, call her mother!'
Soon I'm lying on the couch with my kitten
'No playing out for you'
'Awww!'

Chloe Cripps (8)
St Thomas More RC Primary School, Middleton

Funny Mornings

One sunny morning in the first day of February
The sun was singing gaily
And the flowers were shining brightly.

My mum was inside hoovering the garden,
Dad was outside cleaning the TV,
I was downstairs in my bedroom
When suddenly I saw a house
10 miles away, in front of me!

Jessica Newton (8)
St Thomas More RC Primary School, Middleton

My Grandad

One sunny morning
On a cold winter's day,
I saw my grandad,
Only five years of age.

His house had three floors,
'A bungalow,' he said.
He was poor all over,
With a plasma in each room.

He was happy every day,
But sad seven days a week.
His bed a four poster,
A sheet on the floor.

At the weekend I never see him,
It always makes me cry.
I say goodbye on Friday
Then I say goodbye to you!

Elizabeth Stockton (8)
St Thomas More RC Primary School, Middleton

Sand Poem

Sand in my sandals
Sand in my sandwiches
Sand in my hair
Sand in my teeth
Sand is everywhere I go
Sand is at home
Sand goes up my nose
Sand is at the seaside
Sand is in my ears
Sand gets on my nerves.

Victoria Philbin (8)
St Thomas More RC Primary School, Middleton

Days Of The Week

Monday's a fun day
Playing in the sun day.

Tuesday's a blues day
What kind should I wear today?

Wednesday's a hen's day
Feeding chicks and hens day.

Thursday's a fur day
Stroking a cat's silky fur day.

Friday's a cry day
Crying for your mum day.

Saturday's a batter day
Battering your sister day.

Sundays are like Monday
Just another fun day!

Hooray!

Jake Curran-Pipe (8)
St Thomas More RC Primary School, Middleton

Ghosts!

Ghosts in the basement,
Ghosts in the street,
Ghosts flying all around
And tickling my feet.
Ghosts in my bedroom,
Ghosts in the hall,
Ghosts playing tennis
And chasing the ball.
Ghosts dunking apples,
Ghosts dunking pears,
Ghosts are eating pumpkin seeds,
But nobody cares!

Hannah Morson (10)
St Thomas More RC Primary School, Middleton

Dancers

Dance, dance the night away
Then comes the morning, sway, sway!
I'm dancing here, I'm a dancer.

Watch those dancers, tap their feet.
Oh, look at them clap to the beat,
I want to be a dancer too!

I've put together a dance.
It will put you in a trance.
I like being a dancer.

Now I'm in a dancing show!
In my hair is a lovely pink bow!
Everybody likes my dances!

Can you twirl?
If you can, you can whirl!
Know these steps and you're a dancer!

Have you on a smile not a grin?
Smile and no grin nor sin!
Smile to be a dancer!

Charlotte Stockton (8)
St Thomas More RC Primary School, Middleton

Love

Love is red
It is the smell of fresh roses
Love tastes like fire
It sounds calm
It feels very soft
It lives in a kind heart.

Clare Rusk (9)
St Thomas More RC Primary School, Middleton

Andrew Toomer

Andrew Toomer
Made a hoover
Andrew Toomer
Said, 'That's cool!'

Andrew Toomer
Spreading a rumour
Andrew Toomer
Said, 'That's mad.'

Andrew Toomer
Polished his hoover
Andrew Toomer
Said, 'That's clean.'

Andrew Toomer
Sucked on a Soother
Andrew Toomer
Said, 'That's better.'

Andrew Toomer
Is a fooler
Andrew Toomer
Said, 'No I'm not!'

Andrew Toomer
Stopped the rumour
Andrew Toomer
Said, 'That's all right.'

Andrew Toomer!

Phillip Burke (10)
St Thomas More RC Primary School, Middleton

My Dad

My dad is a squashy beanbag and a bright lamp,
He's a cheetah running for Britain and a seating zebra,
The smell of a rose, the sound of a bird in danger,
A light rain, a sweet taste of a cake, a lucky charm.

Joachim Miller (10)
St Thomas More RC Primary School, Middleton

My Friend Katie

A toy ready to be played with,
A cupboard ready to keep a secret!
She's an elephant who will always remember your feelings,
She's a sly fox who always has a plan to help me.
A history museum,
A Tudor house that will last forever,
A stereo that can be loud or quiet,
A cry of laughter,
A funny April fool's day,
A juicy apple with juicy gossip.

Stephanie Lyons (9)
St Thomas More RC Primary School, Middleton

Fear

Fear is black,
It smells like it's burnt and shaking,
Fear tastes soft and wet,
It sounds like people screaming and frozen with fear,
It feels like shaking people and running faster,
Fear lives in the soul of a haunted house.

Jonathan Mulligan (9)
St Thomas More RC Primary School, Middleton

Freedom

Freedom is light blue,
It smells like grass, flowers and trees,
It tastes like fruit,
It sounds like birds singing,
It feels like a warm breeze,
It lives in the forest between the trees.

Matthew Whittaker (10)
St Thomas More RC Primary School, Middleton

Sometimes

Sometimes I like to see
What's on my TV.

Chocolate is my favourite food,
It always puts me in a good mood.

I'll go for a walk,
When my friends come round we'll have a talk.

Dad makes me laugh
And helps me with my maths and English.

I go shopping with my mum,
It's always lots and lots of fun.

But just being with my family and having a rest
Is really what I like doing best.

Jasmine Davies (9)
St Thomas More RC Primary School, Middleton

I Hate

I hate buzzy bees
just like silly beans
don't like wiggly worms
they make me squirm

I hate buzzing wasps
just like sizzling sauce
don't like slithering snails
make me grow a tail

I hate slithering snakes
just like baking cakes
don't like slimy slugs
they make me want to hunt a bug.

Olivia Coghlan (10)
St Thomas More RC Primary School, Middleton

Justin Timberlake

Justin Timberlake
Ate his finger cake
Justin Timberlake
Said, 'That's nice.'

Justin Timberlake
Fished in a lovely lake
Justin Timberlake
Said, 'That's fun!'

Justin Timberlake
Made a birthday cake
Justin Timberlake
Said, 'That's good!'

Justin Timberlake
Skated on a frozen lake
Justin Timberlake
Said, 'That's hard.'

Justin Timberlake
Said, 'That's a nice day.'

Mitchell Cain (9)
St Thomas More RC Primary School, Middleton

Something's Moving

And something's moving
Even I would be scared of that
Sometimes you see a bat
A big, stiff cupboard
Nasty, wide costumes
A small, old cowboy hat
Up in the attic.

Harris Faulkner (10)
St Thomas More RC Primary School, Middleton

I Like

I like chocolate cake
Just like my mates
But I really
Dislike sprouts.

I like biscuits
With chocolate on top
But I really
Hate some vegetables.

I hate cauliflower
It makes me sick
But I like chocolate
Like everyone else.

Victoria Waters (10)
St Thomas More RC Primary School, Middleton

Peace

Peace is blue.
It smells like roses and tulips.
It tastes like strawberries and cream.
It's the sound of birds tweeting in the sun.
It feels like green fields and the sun.
And lives in the heart of a beautiful garden.

Stephen Maryniak (10)
St Thomas More RC Primary School, Middleton

Pirate Jack

There was a pirate named Jack
And both his eyes were black
He fell on his back
And then it went crack
And he offered me a pint or three.

Sophie Carey (10)
St Thomas More RC Primary School, Middleton

Lucy

My mum is always saying,
'Wash your face.
Clean your teeth.
Lucy, go to bed.
Tidy your room.
Do your hair.'
My mum is so annoying.
My dad is always saying,
'Shut up, I'm watching tele.
Go on a diet, you've got a big belly.
You're not going on holiday,
I don't like you anyway.
Have you got ants
In your pants?
Get me two beers,
Do I see tears?
Lucy, *Lucy!*'

Lucy Rhodes (9)
St Thomas More RC Primary School, Middleton

I Really Love . . .

I really love candy,
I really hate school,
There's a new flavoured yoghurt, it's really cool,
It tastes like apple, it tastes like pie,
And my mum says, 'Cheap stuff, my, my, my.'

I really love candy,
I really hate school,
There is now a better candy, it tastes like gruel,
My mum goes tough
It's too much money, besides it's tacky old stuff!

Mason Matlock (10)
St Thomas More RC Primary School, Middleton

Once There Lived . . .

Once there lived a ghost
Who stole everyone's toast
He came out at night
He scared the daylight
And gave the children a fright.

Once there lived a knight
Who had a black and white kite
At night he came out to fight
He gave them all a fright.

Once there lived a lady
Who loved Slim Shady
She was very much of a baby!

Sean Bamforth (8)
St Thomas More RC Primary School, Middleton

Kindness is . . .

Kindness is sky-blue,
It smells like perfume,
It tastes like sweets and chocolate,
It sounds like a water fountain dripping into a pond,
It feels like a fluffy dog,
It lives in the snowy mountaintops.

Bria Sagar (10)
St Thomas More RC Primary School, Middleton

Limerick

There was an old man from Calcutta
Who slipped and fell down the gutter
He made a big crack
And he broke his back
That silly old man from Calcutta.

Adam Bowler (10)
St Thomas More RC Primary School, Middleton

Up In The Attic

A something's weeping
An old wrecked cupboard
But who?
And someone left it there
A little teddy of Winnie the Pooh
A rusty looking rocking horse
A dusty, old shoe
Up in the attic.

Down in the cellar
A china pot doll
Some rotted, mouldy bread
A picture of Mum
A tattered old bed
Some colourful snakeskin
A rusted statue head
And something's sleeping.

Joseph Beaumont (9)
St Thomas More RC Primary School, Middleton

What I Like And Hate

I like soccer
I like soccer
I hope you do
Because it's cool

I hate ginger cake
I hate finger cake
But I like to bake

I don't go to Scouts
And
I hate Brussels sprouts

I like sweets
I like sweets
They're my treats.

Matthew Hayes (9)
St Thomas More RC Primary School, Middleton

I'm Stuck!

I'm all alone, or am I?
Minute by minute I'm getting more scared.
Scared I'll die of hunger.
The thought of home is a distant memory.
Inhuman is the life I'm leading now.
Crazy! Crazy! I'm starting to become.
Keep me from dying please, now!

Katie Carey (10)
St Thomas More RC Primary School, Middleton

Life

The colour of life is a dark cream like the far, far end
of the sky on a dull morning.
The smell of life is a sweet bar of chocolate, or petrol,
depending on what mood you are in.
The taste of life is a juicy apple in your mouth.
The sound of life is drifting music in the air.
The feel of life is joy, like when a baby is born.

Andrew Murray (9)
St Thomas More RC Primary School, Middleton

Youth

Youth is the colour blue
And smells like a field of flowers
Youth tastes like sweet sugar
And sounds like a sweet baby
Youth feels very smooth
And lives in a house with a family.

Chloe Vergine (10)
St Thomas More RC Primary School, Middleton

Fear

Fear is grey,
It smells like rats' droppings,
It tastes like cold bitter,
It sounds like a dragon's scream,
It feels sharp and hard,
It lives in the deepest, darkest forest.

David Murray (9)
St Thomas More RC Primary School, Middleton

Love

Love is pink,
Love smells of roses,
It tastes like sweet ice cream,
Love sounds like an angel singing,
It feels like a soft cushion,
Love lives right in the middle of your heart.

Hannah Hayes (10)
St Thomas More RC Primary School, Middleton

The Poem Of Fear

Fear is dark and black
It smells like a sewer, all dirty and green
Fear tastes like flesh and blood
It sounds like a wailing ghost being murdered
Fear feels like sharp spikes digging into your skin
Fear lives in your heart and only comes out when you are in danger.

Peter Busby (9)
St Thomas More RC Primary School, Middleton

Pancake

In the dark alleyway
I see a beggar man

Tryin' to make a pancake
With a frying pan

He kicks it
He boots it
He flicks it
He shoots it

He toots at it
He throws it
He bins it
He knows it

It comes back
He hates it
Rubbish is what
He rates it.

James Candlin (10)
St Thomas More RC Primary School, Middleton

Easter

I like Easter
The little rabbit and the chicks too
I like Easter
The flowers, bright and beautiful
The squirrels sit in the trees
Most of all I like my yummy chocolate egg.

Lois Cassin (8)
St Thomas More RC Primary School, Middleton

Stars

The stars are so bright
They light up Mars

They stars are so bright
They crash cars

When stars come too close
They look like a spaceship from Mars

The spaceship from Mars
Left all Mars bars behind
I was the first to get them
The spaceship went back to Mars
I said to myself, 'What would we do without stars?'

Benedict Miller (8)
St Thomas More RC Primary School, Middleton

Limerick

There once was a girl from York
Who tried to eat peas with a fork
They rolled round and round
They bounced on the ground
She decided she was safer with pork.

Christian Walters (10)
St Thomas More RC Primary School, Middleton

Lighthouse

I'm here, you're not
Rocks ahead
Go around, be safe
Or have bad luck
Take my advice and stop.

Joseph Craven (10)
St Thomas More RC Primary School, Middleton

Untidy Room

When my mum came upstairs
To put me to sleep
She said, 'Why are your clothes
In an untidy heap?'

The next night when my mum came
To put me to bed
She said, 'Why all over the floor
Is there grey pencil lead?'

The next night when my mum came
To read me a book
She said, 'There is make-up all over the floor,
Look!'

The next night when
My dad told me that
Mum was at work
He said, 'Why is there water
In a cup on the floor,
Slurp?'

In the morning when my
Mum woke me up, she said,
'Can I see mess? Hey, you, is
It tidy? Yes!'

Stephanie Caldecott (9)
Stansfield Road Junior School

The Sun

When the boiling sun
Shines on my head
It brings light to the world today

When it is midday
It is hotter than before
Midday turns to night.

Jordan Proctor (9)
Stansfield Road Junior School

What Do You Do?

What do you do?
Do you go shopping, play or go to school
or go out with your friends and be cool?

What do you do?
Play swinging on your swing or go on your rollerblades
always get presents on your favourite days?

What do you do?
Jog, walk, or do you run
or are you fat and eat a bun?

What do you do?
Draw, chalk or maybe paint?
For school you don't want to be late.

What do you do?
Excellent, good, but don't be rough
it will be worse if you will be tough.

Alex Davison (8)
Stansfield Road Junior School

Fluffy Snow

The fluffy snow is as delicate as a cloud
The people laugh like hyenas
And the soft white sheet of snow covers the snowman
Who is as round as a football
I see my reflection as the trees are shining like transparent glass
A dog spins round like a twister making snow splat in my face
But tomorrow the snow all be gone
For the blazing sun will turn it to slush
What a winter to remember
Now let me take a picture.

Jonathan Sharrock (8)
Stansfield Road Junior School

Creative Writing

My poem began on Monday,
We looked at a poem called 'Rat-a-tat-tat',
Then someone shouted, out, 'Who is that?'

On Tuesday, my story began,
It started in a spooky castle,
I thought to myself, *I can't stand this hassle.*

On Wednesday, my poem ended,
The door flew open and in he pounded,
The teacher said, 'That's it, boy, you're grounded.'

On Thursday, my story ended,
The ghouls and ghosts flew out into the open,
The castle was closed, not a word to be spoken.

Sophie Brooks (8)
Stansfield Road Junior School

The Snowing Rhyme

Sally sledges as fast as light
Through the snow which is extremely bright
Silly Sam runs faster than a tornado
Round until he feels he's not on the ground
Skidding Savannah goes faster than a cheetah
So nobody can ever beat her
Skating Sean goes up like the sun
And in every race he's actually won
Slippery Shannon slips on the ice that's like glass
But very bad luck it can't take her mass
So they have lots of fun
Why don't you have fun with Sean who's always won?

Chelsea Seale (8)
Stansfield Road Junior School

One Snowy Day

In the snow-time people go ice skating
You cannot see the grass, it is as tiny as can be
There's robins that fly high in the sky like a big tower
Sally slides as fast as can be
Watch her zooming past like a rocket
As the little boy throws snowballs as round as a football
While her dog zoomed too, like a little rocket.

Olivia Willoughby (8)
Stansfield Road Junior School

The Thick Snow

The snow is as thick as a stick.
And the hills are as white as fluffy clouds.
The ice is as white as stained glass.
The bird is as little as a leaf.
The dog is spinning as fast as a propeller.
The snow is as thick as smoke.

Liam Paull (8)
Stansfield Road Junior School

Raw Snow Snow

Snow, snow, you're so slow
Ice, ice, you're too slippy
Faster than a flash
Quicker than lightning
Snowballs going everywhere
We are skating faster than anyone
Snowmen everywhere.

Jamie Wetton (8)
Stansfield Road Junior School

Wars

In 1914 World War I began:
people in trenches,
not even benches to sit on.

In 1939, World War II began:
first there was the Blitz,
bombs smashing houses,
it was the pits.

And there was the war in the Pacific:
the Americans said it was terrific,
the Japanese were on their knees,
praying for the Americans to go.

Then there was Vietnam:
good old Uncle Sam,
followed by the war in the Gulf,
there was no proof,
that weapons were involved.

Last and not least:
there was the police,
stopping war in Oldham.

Thomas Warburton (9)
Stansfield Road Junior School

About My Family

Dolphins are as kind as my mum,
My mum is as sweet as rum.

Monkeys are as cheeky as my dad,
My dad can be mad!

Sharks are amazing as my brother,
My brother is just like my mother.

Dolphins are funny as my Auntie Sue,
I'm going camping with her, whoo!

Kayley Leasley (8)
Stansfield Road Junior School

The Days Of The Week

Monday brings the rain
I can't go out to play again.

Tuesday brings me lots of sweets
These I really like to eat.

Wednesday brings the sun and rain
My sister is a pain.

Thursday brings the snow
The fire has a warm glow.

Friday brings the twinkling stars
Shining bright from afar.

Sunday brings the calm and rest
We all dress in our Sunday best.

Amy Grogan (8)
Stansfield Road Junior School

Winter Wonderland

The grass was as small as a pin,
Over there's little robin,
Sally's sliding very fast,
Watch out, she's zooming past,
The snowballs were as round as footballs,
The boy who's throwing them is extremely tall,
The boy had a bright green shirt,
But was he the snow expert?
The robin had a bright red chest,
She flew quicker than the rest,
And now this poem is nearly done,
Let's shout, *'Have fun everyone!'*

Megan Ashton (8)
Stansfield Road Junior School

D.A.Y.S

My story on Monday began:
Wind and cold in the seas
And underneath my shaking knees.
The teacher wrote a little note,
'Remember your handwriting please!'
My poem on Tuesday began:
That man is terribly crazy
That's why he is so lazy.
The teacher wrote a little note,
'Why is he so lazy?'
My poem on Wednesday began:
On the day I was born
It was such a yawn,
The teacher wrote a little note,
'What has happened to that full stop?'
My story on Thursday began:
Why don't you run along or sing a little song?
The teacher wrote a little note,
'Why did he sing a song?'
My story on Friday began:
Why does my teacher have to be the boss
And why is she always so cross?
The teacher wrote a little note,
'I am not the boss and I am never cross!'

Laura Cotterill (9)
Stansfield Road Junior School

Faster And Faster

Silly Sally's dog ran faster than the speed of light
The tree is like an ice cream waving side to side
The dog is whizzing round and round
Faster than you can see. If you whizz around
Too much, you will start to come around.

Kelly-Anne Western (8)
Stansfield Road Junior School

What Do You Do?

What do you do?
Collect coins, play all sorts of games
Or skip away with someone who has never seen?

What do you do?
Sing, laugh and play all sorts of jokes
Or play with everyone by softly poking?

What do you do?
Bang your head, play hide-and-seek
Or one of Mum's necklaces, secretly sneak?

What do you do?
Scream, collect photographs of dogs
Or keep Christmas cards from your mates?

What do you do?

Rebecca Lear (8)
Stansfield Road Junior School

Snow Is Fun

Skating Sally slid all day
It was free, so she didn't have to pay
She slid, slid and slid all day
And she wasted no money
Case, the lawyer, paid each day
She loved to skate
Sally slid, slid and slid
Faster, faster than the speed of light
Sean ran through the ground
When Sally's dog came bouncing round
Sally skates, Sally skated faster, faster
She shouted *bang!* she fell down.

Stephanie Macpherson (8)
Stansfield Road Junior School

My Picture

My picture on Monday was like:
XIII carrying a lock pick,
And instead of drawing someone sick,
I'd rather draw someone thick.

My picture on Tuesday was like:
The President and his wife,
Holding a butcher's knife,
Before I thought of drawing a fight.

My picture on Wednesday was like:
A man with a lollipop,
The man had a really red top,
After Ammiel made a noise like *'pop!'*

My picture on Thursday was like:
A tree falling on a shed,
After I got hit on the head,
I'm really hungry, 'I want to be fed!'

My picture on Friday was like:
A sweet little bird humming a tune,
Then I drew a picture of a roller coaster tycoon,
The day will finally be over . . . soon.

Curtis Newton (8)
Stansfield Road Junior School

Pink Rabbit

The rabbit has fur like a pink flower.
The eyes are as red as roses and tulips.
His ears are as big as a sunflower.
His nose is like a big button.

Savannah Dean (9)
Stansfield Road Junior School

Days

On Monday:
It was my first day at school,
The next day I'm going to the swimming pool

On Tuesday:
I went swimming,
And played water polo, and my team was winning

On Wednesday:
I could hear the school bell ringing,
Ran into the hall and children singing

On Thursday:
It is maths until lunch,
But all the children go *munch, munch, munch*

On Friday:
It is golden time,
All the way until home time.

Sam James (9)
Stansfield Road Junior School

Best Day For Snow

The dog is spinning round and round and round,
and round, he is not touching the ground,
seeing lots of colourful skates on his way,
running down and down seeing nothing but a blur,
Sally speeding down, shouting and laughing,
as she's going down the icy snow,
enjoying her time with her friends,
she thinks the sun will shine and
beam on the ice so it will all go.

Daniel Merrington (9)
Stansfield Road Junior School

Successful Days

Monday is a school day,
We have to do a poem,
Anyway I've got mine done,
And I think it was a lot of fun.

Wednesday, I have to do a story,
It was so good, I'm so happy,
I've won best presentation,
My teacher said I've won the competition.

Friday, I have won a certificate,
It says that I am good,
So now I am so happy,
And my teacher says that I will succeed.

Emma Lowe (9)
Stansfield Road Junior School

The Snow Is Falling

The snow is cold, it freezes everything.
Skiing in the snow, it's all around.
Skiing in the snow.
Everybody's gloves are bright.
Sally's gloves are yellow and very bright like the sun.
The brown dog is spinning fast like a tornado.
The snowman's buttons are round like a clock.
The rabbit's eyes are as red as a shiny apple.
And when the snowman was built you could hear him cackle.
While sleepy Sean and super Shannon
Slide down the hill on their
Snowboards sliding and slipping.

Shannon Lewis (9)
Stansfield Road Junior School

My Life In Days

Monday brings the treats
like magazines and sweets

Tuesday, I've got to feed my rabbits
it's a pain to get the carrots

Wednesday is the middle
I've got to play upon my fiddle

Thursday is almost at the end
it drives me mad and round the bend

Friday is the end of the week
it makes my brother shout and shriek.

Charlotte Ingham (8)
Stansfield Road Junior School

Winter Winter

When it is winter, it is as cold as ice,
When it is winter, it is so cold, the poor mice.
When it is winter, it is really fun!
When it is winter, there is no sun.

The ice is as transparent as glass,
Run over there, you can see the class.
Silly Sarah snowboarding around,
I've got a feeling she'll hit the ground!
Stupid Sam throwing snowballs,
It does not matter, he hits the walls!

Jenny Britain
Stansfield Road Junior School

My Adventures

My adventure on Monday began;
a princess, a castle, a huge trial,
and a king and queen with a crown,
my mum woke me up, 'Victoria, come down.'
My adventure on Tuesday began;
a monster in dark caves,
that growled fiercely and scarily,
my mum shouted, I got out of bed wearily.
My adventure on Wednesday began;
the drifting love happened to come,
with a kiss from a prince, my friend said, 'Wake up,'
I haven't loved since.
My adventure on Thursday began;
a cold, misty day, so cold I froze,
my mum woke me up,
'Take those socks off your toes.'
My adventure on Friday began;
me wishing for school not to come,
my mum woke me up,
'It'll be fun.'

Victoria Aldred (8)
Stansfield Road Junior School

Snow Snow

Snow snow, white, white snow.
Snow is as white as a diamond.
You can slide in snow, play in snow.
It's really cold, it tickles my toes, the wind blows.
When the children throw snowballs like lightning.

Jordan Oliver (8)
Stansfield Road Junior School

The War

The war on Monday began:
Strong tanks battled for victory,
The PlayStation crashed just at my shot,
I stood up and shouted, 'Thanks a lot!'

The war began again on Tuesday:
The wires were hanging out,
I couldn't do a thing but shout,
It looks like it's in a mix.

The war ended on Wednesday, I think:
I shot and killed their boss,
'I won,' I said, with a shout,
But my brother came in and wiped it out!

The war was on again on Thursday against my brother:
I kicked and punched,
But in the end I got thumped,
'I give in, right, it's the end!'

The war was over on Friday:
The war was over, the PlayStation was broken,
Now I have to play with puppets,
But at least I can call my brother a muppet!

Jack Bromley (8)
Stansfield Road Junior School